TOP 10 SEATTLE

ERIC AMRINE

Left **Pike Place Market piggy bank** Center **Experience Music Project** Right **Laguna pottery**

LONDON, NEW YORK,
MELBOURNE, MUNICH AND DELHI
www.dk.com

Reproduced by Colourscan, Singapore
Printed and bound by South China Printing Co. Ltd, China

First American Edition, 2005

07 08 09 10 9 8 7 6 5 4 3 2 1

Published in the United States by DK Publishing, Inc., 375 Hudson Street New York, New York 10014

Reprinted with revisions 2007

ISSN: 1479-344X
ISBN: 978-0-75660-901-6

Within each Top 10 list in this book, no hierarchy of quality or popularity is implied. All 10 are, in the editor's opinion, of roughly equal merit.

Contents

Seattle's Top 10

The information in this DK Eyewitness Top 10 Travel Guide is checked regularly.

Every effort has been made to ensure that this book is as up-to-date as possible at the time of going to press. Some details, however, such as telephone numbers, opening hours, prices, gallery hanging arrangements and travel information are liable to change. The publishers cannot accept responsibility for any consequences arising from the use of this book, nor for any material on third party websites, and cannot guarantee that any website address in this book will be a suitable source of travel information. We value the views and suggestions of our readers very highly. Please write to: Publisher, DK Eyewitness Travel Guides, Dorling Kindersley, 80 Strand, London, Great Britain WC2R 0RL.

Cover: **Corbis**: Bill Ross main; Joel W. Rogers bl; **DK Images:** Scott Pitts cl;
Spine: **DK Images:** Scott Pitts; Back: **Corbis**: Paul A. Souders r; **DK Images**: Gunter Marx l; Scott Pitts
© Jonathon Borofsky *Hammering Man* c.

Left **Alki Beach** Right **University of Washington**

Left **Washington State Ferry on Puget Sound** Right **Seattle Art Museum**

Key to abbreviations
Adm *admission charge* **Free** *no admission charge* **Dis. access** *disabled access*

SEATTLE'S TOP 10

TOP 10 Seattle Highlights

Over the last decade, Seattle has blossomed into a bustling powerhouse of influence, steering the future of high technology as well as popular culture. The population of this vibrant metropolis is fueled by the latest in software, espresso drinks, music, and visual art that's often as far on the leading edge as the city itself. Seattle has emerged as one of the most attractive cities in the United States, with an ever-changing skyline that reflects the pioneering spirit that brought settlers here in the mid-19th century.

1 Pike Place Market
An integral part of the Seattle experience, visitors flock to this thriving landmark all year round. Explore the invigorating mix of fresh seafood, farmers' produce, flower stalls, and ethnic foods *(see pp8–9)*.

2 Seattle Center
The site of the 1962 World's Fair, the Center is now entirely dedicated to the pursuit of arts and entertainment. While many original edifices remain – the Space Needle being the most recognized – the location also inspires new building designs, such as Frank Gehry's Experience Music Project *(see pp10–11)*.

3 Elliott Bay Waterfront
Seattle is a major port for both industrial and passenger traffic. Sights along Puget Sound's Elliott Bay include pier shops and restaurants just blocks from towering industrial cranes loading containers onto freighters *(see pp12–13)*.

4 Pioneer Square

A treasure trove of Victorian-era architecture and streets still paved with bricks or cobblestone, Seattle's original commercial center was established in 1852 when Aurthur A. Denny and David Denny arrived with a handful of fellow pioneers. This is now a protected National Historic District *(see pp14–15)*.

5 International District
The ID, as locals call it, is a mélange of Chinese, Korean, Japanese, and Southeast Asian cultures. Seattle's Pacific Rim identity makes it a final destination for émigrés from across the Pacific *(see pp16–17)*.

Previous pages **Seattle skyline with Space Needle in the forefront**

6 Broadway

A summer night along Capitol Hill's main strip can resemble midtown Manhattan in terms of lively street scenes. Expect the unexpected – outrageous attire and flamboyant behavior *(see pp18–19)*.

7 Lake Washington Ship Canal

Officially completed in 1934, the Canal bisects the city and provides access to the sea for pleasure boaters, research vessels, and commercial barges alike *(see pp20–21)*.

Green Lake
Green Lake Park
PHINNEY AVE N
AURORA AVENUE N
NE 65TH STREET
ROOSEVELT WAY NE
11TH AVENUE NE
35TH AVENUE NE
9
N 50TH ST
MARKET STREET
45TH ST N
University District
45TH STREET NE
Fremont
Wallingford
8
NE PACIFIC STREET
MONTLAKE BLVD NE
University of Washington Parklands
NICKERSON ST
N 34TH ST
Union Bay
7
Eastlake
Montlake
Lake Union
WESTLAKE AVENUE
FAIRVIEW AVENUE N
Lake View Cemetery Volunteer Park
24TH AVENUE E
LAKE WASHINGTON BLVD
Lake Washington Arboretum
Japanese Garden
QUEEN ANNE AVE N
Belltown
Capitol Hill
6
15TH AVENUE E
W MERCER STREET
E MADISON STREET
2
BROAD STREET
E OLIVE WAY
DENNY WAY
BROADWAY
Downtown
Madrona
23RD AVENUE E
1
BOREN AVENUE
14TH AVENUE
Central District
Elliott Bay
3
YESLER WAY
23RD AVENUE S
4
4TH AVENUE S
5
1 miles 0 km 1

8 University of Washington

One of the nation's top universities, UW comprises a student body of nearly 40,000, an attractive campus, and huge endowments from local benefactors in the high-tech industry *(see pp22–23)*.

9 Woodland Park Zoo

The design of Seattle's world-class zoo affords its animals vast enclosures. Natural habitats surround the viewing areas and pathways snake through its 92 acres *(see pp24–25)*.

10 Discovery Park

Rising above Puget Sound is a gorgeous 534-acre park. Densely wooded trails, beaches, historic military homes, and wildlife are just some of its attractive features *(see pp26–27)*.

Top 10 Pike Place Market

Neon fish advertisement

The Market stretches for several blocks high above the port traffic sailing on the gleaming waters of Elliott Bay. This historic district includes a meandering multi-level underground arcade, and street-level tables and stalls. Established in 1907, America's oldest continually operating farmers' market has become one of Seattle's most treasured institutions. By mid-century, most farmers' tables were run by Japanese-Americans, and their tragic internment during World War II nearly ended the market's operation. Plans to raze the old buildings fortunately ceased in 1971, when architect Victor Steinbrueck and his supporters saved them from the wrecking ball.

Famous neon cup sign

The market abounds in ethnic foods. Three Girls Bakery offers freshly baked bread and tasty sandwiches. For delicious in-door dining, head to Il Bistro for Italian, Place Pigalle for French urban, or Café Campagne for French country cuisine.

- *Map J4*
- *Between Pike & Virginia St, from 1st to Western Ave; (206) 682-7453; www.pikeplacemarket.org*
- *Open daily except Thanksgiving, Christmas & New Year's Day.*
- *Three Girls Bakery: 1514 Pike St; (206) 622-1045*
- *DeLaurenti's: 1435 1st Ave; 1-800-873-6685*

Top 10 Sights

1. Pike Place Fish Company
2. Starbucks
3. Steinbrueck Park
4. Underground Mezzanines
5. Buskers
6. Organic Wednesdays
7. DeLaurenti's
8. Hillclimb
9. Hmong Flower Stalls
10. Read All About It

1 Pike Place Fish Company

Crowds and film crews gather to witness these entertaining fishmongers *(right)*. Their skills include hurling fish high over customers and countertops to be weighed, filetted, and wrapped for travel.

2 Starbucks

The West was won with steamed milk and dark roast coffee. Howard Schultz's global retail coffee empire began right here in 1971, at Starbucks' first store *(above)*.

3 Steinbrueck Park

Its wonderful grassy hill makes this a popular lunch destination. Pack a picnic, find a spot, and drink in the gorgeous views of Puget Sound, the Olympic Mountains, and Seattle's skyline.

4 Underground Mezzanines

Follow a maze of ramps and stairways to reach this shopping wonderland. Browse collectibles and books, have your palm read, commission a portrait, or treat yourself to local arts and crafts.

Summer Saturdays are the Market's busiest days. For a more leisurely visit, try a weekday morning.

7 DeLaurenti's

Step inside to sample the delicious offerings of this Mediterranean gourmet grocery. Fresh breads and cheese, and a large wine selection create a great summer picnic.

5 Buskers

Street music *(above)* is a constant feature of the Market life. You might catch the hyperkinetic show of a spoons player who featured in at least one award-winning rock video, or be entertained by gospel quartets, piano troubadours, or a kazoo soloist.

9 Hmong Flower Stalls

Seattle's small, entrepreneurial SE Asian Hmong community dominates the Market's flower stalls. You can smell the blossoms from oversized bouquets even before seeing them through the crowds. In winter, residents make do with equally colorful dry flowers.

10 Read All About It

This quaint, old-fashioned newsstand *(below)* offers a wide array of newspapers and magazines from around the world.

8 Hillclimb

This enclosed stairway and elevator connects the Market to the waterfront and more stores and restaurants in between. It also offers enchanting sea-to-mountain views *(below)*.

6 Organic Wednesdays

Check out the Market's Wednesday program during the spring and fall harvests *(above)*. Look for the yellow ribbon surrounding a block-long stretch dedicated to the produce of Washington's organic farmers.

Rachel the Pig

Don't miss Rachel, Seattle's largest piggy bank. This brassy icon of the Market Foundation also serves as the Market's sentry at the main entrance. All proceeds from visitors' donations to Rachel go towards low-income groups.

Don't try driving through crowded Pike Place. Instead, use the parking lots on Western Avenue, then take a walking tour.

TOP 10 Seattle Center

The site of 1962's Century 21 Exposition, tagged "America's Space Age World's Fair," Seattle Center has survived decades of massive growth all around it. The main attraction is still the Space Needle, revealing the futuristic vision of 1960's Seattle. Today, a close second is the ultra-modern and controversial Experience Music Project, Paul Allen's monument to rock music. For the city's residents, the Center is synonymous with lavish presentations of art, theater, dance, and music all year long.

Experience Music Project

Seattle Center

Space Needle, Seattle's official landmark

While the Center House contains many restaurants, walk along Queen Anne Ave for a wider selection, including Thai restaurants. For baked goods and espresso, try Uptown Espresso & Bakery, 525 Queen Anne Ave N (206) 285-3757

- *Map H2*
- *Seattle Center: (206) 684-7200; www.seattle-center.com*
- *Space Needle: $14.00 adults, $7 for 4–13; 9am–12am daily*
- *McCaw Hall listings: (206) 684-7200*
- *EMP: (206) 367-5483*
- *Monorail: due to open in mid-2007*
- *KeyArena: (206) 733-9200*
- *Pacific Science Center: 200 2nd Ave N; (206) 443-2001*
- *Seattle Children's Theatre: 201 Thomas St, (206) 441-3322*

Top 10 Sights

1. Space Needle
2. Opera House
3. Experience Music Project
4. Center House
5. Bagley Wright Theatre
6. Monorail
7. Key Arena
8. Bumbershoot
9. Pacific Science Center
10. Seattle Children's Theatre

1 Space Needle

This imposing structure *(see p32)* is recognized as the city's architectural icon. Ride the vintage external elevators to the observation deck for a majestic view, or reserve a table at the revolving Space City restaurant for 360-degree panoramic views while dining.

2 Opera House

The luxurious Marion Oliver McCaw Hall *(below & p38)* is home to the Seattle Opera. The site also contains Café Impromptu and the Boeing plaza.

3 Experience Music Project (EMP)

Paul Allen, co-founder of Microsoft and avid rock aficionado, commissioned distinguished modern architect Frank Gehry to design this technicolor performance venue *(see p32)*. It also houses the new Science Fiction Museum and Hall of Fame.

4 Center House

This large building houses the wonderful Seattle Children's Museum *(see p40)* as well as an intimate theater. It also contains restaurants, cafés, and shops.

Seattle Center used to be a favorite potlatch site for coastal Native Americans until the late 19th century.

5 Bagley Wright Theatre

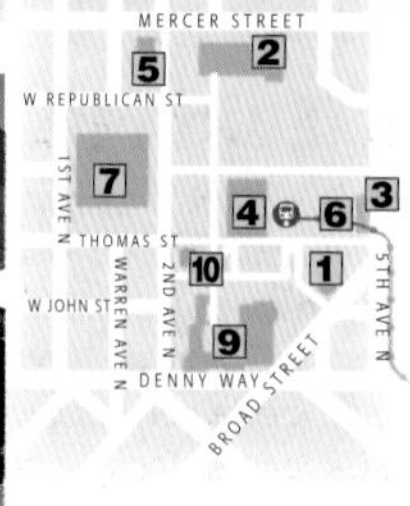

The anchor for the Seattle Repertory Group, the theater rose in 1963 to become a Tony Award-winning playhouse. It is the largest of the three stages the Rep *(right & p38)* operates for their performances.

9 Pacific Science Center

You'll find exhibits on topics such as electronic music making, robotics, hydraulics, and natural history *(below)*. There's also a toddler area and two IMAX theaters.

10 Seattle Children's Theatre (SCT)

An award-winning organization that entertains 260,000 patrons each year. The Charlotte Martin Theater and the Eve Alford Theater are recognized for innovative family-oriented programs.

6 Monorail

Planners of the 1962 World's Fair imagined the future of mass transportation might resemble this train *(right & p32)*. The Monorail has been out of service since a train collision in 2005 and is due to reopen in mid-2007. Plans to extend the route were shelved following a public vote.

7 KeyArena

The largest indoor venue *(below & p38)* in Seattle Center, with events ranging from heavy metal concerts to pro basketball games.

8 Bumbershoot

Seattleites mark their calendars for the long Labor Day holiday weekend in September, when Bumbershoot brings artists and imaginative literary arts programs, musicians, independent films, ethnic food, and many surprises to Seattle Center for the region's largest festival of its kind *(see p34)*.

1962 World's Fair

Century 21's designers demonstrated their vision of the future in 1962, only 50 years after Seattle's first World's Fair, the Alaska-Yukon-Pacific Exhibition. Modernity ruled, from the science-fictionesque Needle and Monorail to the Sputnik-like Center Fountain. Nearly 10 million visitors came to marvel at this ideal future. Even Elvis Presley made an appearance, filming *It Happened at the World's Fair*, (1963). Today, it is considered strictly retro, if not kitsch.

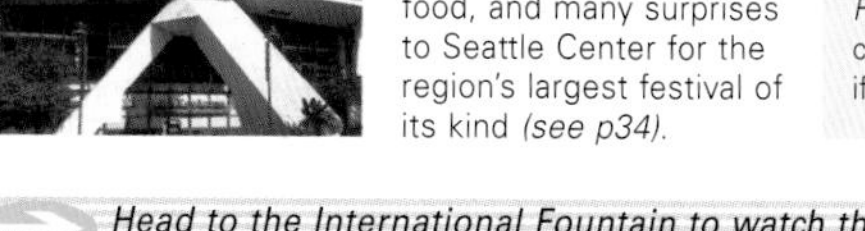

Head to the International Fountain to watch the jets of water pulsing to music and to see kids of all ages getting wet!

Elliott Bay Waterfront

One of Seattle's most distinguishing features is its working waterfront. It is the core of Seattle's thriving maritime community and is chock full of the sights, shore-bird cries, and briny air of a seaport metropolis. It's the place to catch ferries to Bainbridge Island or the Kitsap Peninsula, or view sea life at the Seattle Aquarium. The piers are tourist central, replete with restaurants and bars, import shops, and harbor tours. On the southern end of the bay, acres of container yards border the city's gritty but fascinating industrial district.

Seattle Aquarium

Catch your fresh seafood meal at Anthony's Pier 66 & Bell St Diner, 2201 Alaskan Way, (206) 448-6688, a respected Seattle institution. There's a carry-out section for fish 'n' chips or chowder, a seafood vendor, and an excellent indoor restaurant with dockside seating.

- *Map H4*
- *Ferries Terminal: Pier 52; (206) 464-6400*
- *Seattle Aquarium: Pier 59; (206) 386-4300; Adm; www.seattle aquarium.org*
- *Ye Olde Curiosity Shop: Pier 54; (206) 682-5844; 9am–9:30pm daily*
- *Odyssey Maritime Discovery Center: Bell St Pier 66; (206) 374-4000; www.ody.org; 10am–3pm Tue–Thu, 10am–4pm Fri, 11am–5pm Sat; Adm $7 adults, $5 seniors/ students*

Top 10 Sights

1. Waterfront Streetcar
2. Washington State Ferries
3. Seattle Aquarium
4. Ye Olde Curiosity Shop
5. Bell Harbor Marina
6. Water Sports & Tours
7. Odyssey Maritime Discovery Center
8. Myrtle Edwards Park
9. Cruise Ship Terminals
10. Container Yards

1 Waterfront Streetcar

Children love this delightful Old World mode of travel along the waterfront *(above)*. Hop aboard at any of nine stations between Myrtle Edwards Park and the International District. They run every 20 minutes.

2 Washington State Ferries

An icon of the Pacific Northwest, these ferries provide a picturesque, inexpensive cruise across Puget Sound, as well as transporting Seattle's commuters from neighboring shores.

3 Seattle Aquarium

The waterfront's most popular all-weather attraction is the world-class Seattle Aquarium. Make a point to step inside the Aquarium's glass-domed room *(below)* under 400,000 gallons of water for spectacular shark and octopus views. Watch divers feed the fish in the Underwater Dome and the sharks in the Coral Reef Exhibit. There are also talks and craft activities for children.

CityPass offers admission to multiple attractions such as Seattle Aquarium and Argosy Cruises: Adult $42, Child $29 **See p108**

4 Ye Olde Curiosity Shop

Looking for literature etched on rice grains, or other such unique objects? Since 1899, this has been the place *(above)* to find curios both from the distant and recent past. It's also a great source for coastal Native American art.

9 Cruise Ship Terminals

Seattle's relative proximity to Alaska's stunning Inside Passage, coupled with modern trends in leisure travel, led the city to build two new terminals to accommodate the thousands of passengers coming and going. You can watch ships docking by the Bell Harbor Marina all summer long.

5 Bell Harbor Marina

This harbor *(above)* provides moorage for pleasure boats, large and small. It's adjacent to the port of Seattle's cruise-ship terminal.

6 Water Sports & Tours

If you're feeling adventurous, strap on a paraglider and head up for a breathtaking ride and aerial city view. Many boat cruises depart from here.

7 Odyssey Maritime Discovery Center

Celebrating Seattle's working waterfront, this institution *(see p37)* has hands-on exhibits for landlubbers and their kids. You can steer a virtual tanker ship into harbor, try kayaking, spin a tanker's propeller with pedal power, or operate miniature canal locks.

8 Myrtle Edwards Park

Visit this waterfront haven *(left)* for fine views of Mount Rainier, Puget Sound, and the Olympic Mountains. A bike trail and pedestrian path winds along the Elliott Bay coastline. The park also has a fishing pier.

10 Container Yards

Seattle's local economy depends heavily on a successful shipping industry and marine activity predominates here. Constant tanker, tug boat, and rail traffic represent the city's financial well being.

Seafair & Tug Boat Races

One of the most famed summer events is Seafair, a citywide festival that includes the famous tug boat races on Elliott Bay. Neither sleek nor sluggish, these champions of the sea are something to behold *(see p34)*.

For an unparalleled cityscape, pack an extra roll of film and catch a Washington State Ferry to Winslow, returning to Seattle at sunset.

Top 10 Pioneer Square

The birthplace of modern Seattle has a colorful history marked by economic and geological fluctuations. The Great Fire of 1889 virtually destroyed it, before Alaska's Gold Rush breathed new life and Victorian architecture into the mix. The old warehouses and narrow streets gave rise to a thriving loft arts scene in the 1980s and 90s. While rents have skyrocketed and developers continue to renovate the grand façades of relic buildings, the galleries, cafés, and entrepreneurial spirit remain. The district stands as a testament to a city's survival, particularly after a devastating earthquake in 2001.

Cedar totem poles

If the weather's rainy or cold, curl up under high ceilings by Grand Central Bakery's cozy fireplace with a good book and a tasty meal or dessert.

- *Map K5*
- *Elliott Bay Book Co.: 101 S Main St; (206) 624-6600; 9:30am–10pm Mon–Sat, 11am–7pm Sun*
- *Bill Speidel's Underground Tour: 608 1st Ave; (206) 613-3108*
- *Grand Central Bakery: 214 1st Ave S; (206) 622-3644; $*
- *Merchant's Café: 109 Yesler Way; (206) 624-1515*
- *Klondike Gold Rush National Historical Park: 319 2nd Ave S; (206) 220-4240*

Top 10 Sights

1. Smith Tower
2. Elliott Bay Book Company
3. Bill Speidel's Underground Tour
4. First Thursdays
5. Pioneer Square
6. Grand Central Bakery
7. Waterfall Garden
8. Merchant's Café
9. Klondike Gold Rush National Historical Park
10. Skid Road

1 Smith Tower

Built in 1914 by typewriter tycoon L.C. Smith, at 42 stories this skyscraper *(above & p33)* was once the tallest edifice west of New York. Ride the hand-operated elevator to the observation deck for great views.

2 Elliott Bay Book Company

A bibliophile's dream destination *(above)*, this is one of Seattle's best booksellers. Expect an erudite and informed staff, an incredible selection, a large café, and a notable series of author's readings.

3 Bill Speidel's Underground Tour

Deliberately unusual in name and nature, this outfit presents a remarkable look at Pioneer Square's underground history. The Great Fire, tidal patterns, and poor sewage design forced citizens to convert second stories into first, shown through this subterranean 90-minute walk starting from Pioneer Building *(below & p33)*.

4 First Thursdays

On the first Thursday of each month, from 6pm to 8pm, galleries sponsor a well-attended art walk. Patrons can talk directly to the artists about their displayed works. An ideal starting point is Occidental Way between Main and Jackson Street, where you can find many of the galleries *(right)* and upscale shops.

5 Pioneer Square

This cobblestone triangle of land bordered by Yesler Way and First Avenue is notable for a Tlingit totem pole, and a statue of Seattle's namesake, Chief Sealth. It also features an iron-and-glass pergola *(above)* built in 1909 that once marked the entrance to the "finest underground restroom in the United States".

6 Grand Central Bakery

This is the artisinal bakery and café that helped make hand-rolled European-style bread a mainstay in Seattle.

7 Waterfall Garden

In the Northwest, water is everywhere. Step inside this tiny private park to meditate on a man-made paean to tumbling water *(below)*.

8 Merchant's Café

Popular and still prospering after 100 years, Merchant's Café is Seattle's oldest restaurant with Victorian decor and hearty meals.

9 Klondike Gold Rush National Historical Park

A versatile display of exhibits, films, and photographs emphasize Seattle's role as the closest US city to Alaskan gold, and as a crucial supply post for claim stakers *(below & p30)*.

10 Skid Road

Henry Yesler's logging mill sat at the foot of what is now Yesler Way, a hill as long and steep as any in San Francisco. He used it to slide timber down to the wharf. When Pioneer Square's economy tumbled, Skid Road came to signify desolation and despair.

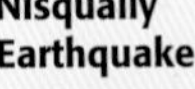

Nisqually Earthquake

In February 2001, Pioneer Square and the entire Puget Sound region experienced a 40-second earthquake, measuring a whopping 6.8 on the Richter scale. Several otherwise sturdy and fireproof brick-and-mortar constructions from post-1889 met their match. Falling bricks and façades crushed cars and damaged many edifices *(see p31)*.

Make a day out of touring both Pioneer Square and the ID (see pp16–17)*; route 99 links these adjacent districts.*

TOP 10 International District

Once known as Chinatown, this district was renamed when community leaders recognized that inhabitants from all over Asia had made that term obsolete. One of Seattle's most historical districts, the ID is a striking example of how Asian cultures thrive and assimilate into Western society. Each ethnicity claims a particular quadrant, even while co-existing in the same colorful part of town. Stroll through groceries and restaurants run by Cambodians, Koreans, Japanese, Vietnamese, and others, to experience the Orient, Pacific Northwest style.

Dragon depicting Asian culture

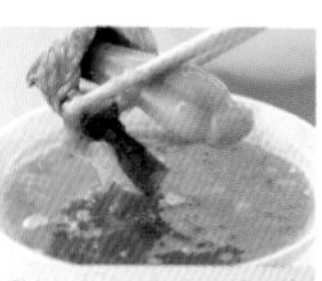

Chinese dipping sauce

For tasty Vietnamese, try Thanh Vi at 1046 S Jackson St, (206) 329-0208. For Chinese, head to Seven Stars Pepper Szechuan Restaurant at 1207 S Jackson St, Suite 211, (206) 568-6446

* *Map L6*
* *ID: (206) 382-1197; www.internationaldistrict.org*
* *Union Station: 501 S. Jackson St; (206) 622-3214*
* *China Gate restaurant: 516 7th Ave; (206) 624-1730*
* *Ocean City: 609 S Weller St; (206) 623-2333*
* *Wing Luke Museum: 407 7th Ave S; (206) 623-5124*
* *Tsue Chong Co Inc.: (206) 623-0801; 9:30am–5am Mon–Fri, 10:30–2pm Sat*
* *Seattle's Best Tea: (206) 749-9855*
* *Uwajimaya: (206) 624-6248*
* *Safeco Field: (206) 346-4000*
* *Qwest Field: (206) 381-7555*
* *Great Wall Mall: 18230 E Valley Hwy, Kent; (425) 251-1600; Daily 9am–9pm*

Top 10 Sights

1. Chinese Lunar New Year
2. Little Saigon
3. Union Station
4. Dim Sum
5. Wing Luke Asian Museum
6. Tsue Chong Company Inc.
7. Seattle's Best Tea
8. Uwajimaya
9. Train Tunnel
10. Safeco Field/Qwest Field

1 Chinese Lunar New Year

A traditional celebration in Chinese communities worldwide, Seattle's version takes place inside the Great Hall of the historic Union Station. Streetside Kung Fu lion dances *(right)*, music, and firework displays make this a festive day for both locals and tourists looking for winter fun in the city.

2 Little Saigon

The storefronts here resemble images of 1960s-era Saigon, with large, bright signage in the native language *(below)*.

3 Union Station

This Beaux Arts-style station *(above)* opened in 1911 with a black and white mosaic floor and a 55-ft (16-m) vaulted ceiling that supports hundreds of lights. It has been sensationally remodeled and is now popular as an event venue.

Avoid parking in the ID on game days at Safeco or Qwest Fields or you'll be fighting crowds on the streets and sidewalks.

4 Dim Sum

Seattle is serious about food, and the crowds flock to the International District for these mandatory Chinese delicacies *(above)*. Excellent choices are China Gate and Ocean City.

6 Tsue Chong Company Inc.

If you smell something sweet amid pungent aromas of the International District, it's likely to be this outfit, which makes delicious noodles and fortune cookies.

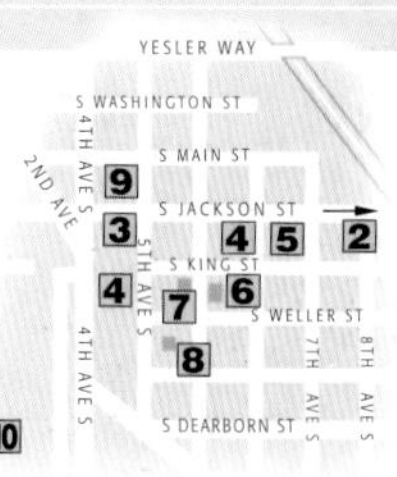

7 Seattle's Best Tea

Tea finds its rightful place in a city overrun by coffee shops. Joe Hsu's small, bright, modern shop is the real deal. Customers can sample the delicious teas. Prices range from $20 to $217 per pound.

9 Train Tunnel

Passenger and freight trains thunder below the edge of the ID. The tunnel ends just past Pike Place Market.

10 Safeco Field/ Qwest Field

Seattle's professional baseball and football teams are based across the street from each other, in the space between International District and Pioneer Square *(above)*.

5 Wing Luke Asian Museum

The vision of civic leader Wing Luke who died in a plane crash in 1965, this museum explores the culture and history of Asian Pacific Americans through a series of permanent and visiting exhibitions *(see p37)*.

8 Uwajimaya

If you can't make it to the Far East, head to the largest Asian market in the Pacific Northwest *(below)*. This store has a vast array of Asian products, merchandise, and a huge ethnic food court offering cuisine from all over Asia.

Great Wall Mall

This 9-acre mall offers an amazing Asian shopping extravaganza. It's a bit of a drive to Kent, which is south of Sea-Tac Airport, but the sheer size and selection of these Asian import stores is worth seeing. Retailers here mirror the local immigrant populations and influences not only from China, but also from all over Asia.

Broadway

This is the main drag that slices across Capitol Hill, one of Seattle's edgier communities just up the hill from downtown. Block after block of hip stores and a wide variety of cafés and restaurants attract a thriving gay culture and gritty youth population. On warm nights, Broadway is about as urban as Seattle gets as it surges with pedestrians. Thanks to the avenue's proclivity for over-the-edge fashion, people-watching can be a year-round activity and great source of entertainment. Broadway has, until recently, served as the main route for the Seattle Pride March (see p72). *The march has now moved out of the area.*

Broadway Performance Hall, Capitol Hill

There are several pockets of panhandlers and homeless street people along Broadway. Use your discretion if asked for donations.

- *Map L3*
- *Broadway Performance Hall; 1625 Broadway (206) 325-3113*
- *Cal Anderson Park/ Lincoln Reservoir: 11th between E Pine/E Denny*
- *Red Light: 312 Broadway Ave E; (206) 329-2200*
- *Bailey/Coy Books: 414 Broadway Ave E; (206) 323-8842*
- *Zebraclub: 421 E Pine St; (206) 325-2452*
- *The Vajra: 518 Broadway Ave E; (206) 323-7846*
- *Dick's: 115 Broadway Ave E; (206) 323-1300*

Top 10 Sights

1. Broadway Performance Hall
2. Jimi Hendrix sculpture
3. Cal Anderson Park
4. Dance Steps on Broadway
5. Red Light
6. Bailey/Coy Books
7. Zebraclub
8. The Vajra
9. Harvard Exit/Egyptian Theaters
10. Dick's

1 Broadway Performance Hall

Originally Broadway High School, the hall *(see p39)* is part of the campus for Seattle Central Community College. Victor Steinbrueck was instrumental in restoring this structure. Its repertoire includes film festivals, and music and dance recitals.

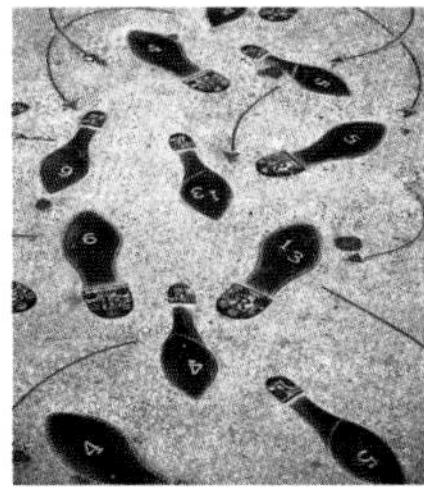

2 Jimi Hendrix sculpture

This cast iron sculpture of rock legend Jimi Hendrix is located by the popular Pike/Pine corridor.

Water sculpture, Cal Anderson Park

3 Cal Anderson Park

Named after one of Washington's openly gay legislators, the park features Lincoln Reservoir, Bobby Morris playfield, tennis courts, a children's play area to the southeast, and an interactive water feature.

4 Dance Steps on Broadway

Sculptor Jack Mackie created an amusing series of inlaid bronze dance steps *(left)* along the sidewalks of Broadway in 1982.

Parking on Capitol Hill is at a premium; leave the car at the hotel and take a bus instead.

5 Red Light

This two-story bastion of quirk and fashion is Seattle's largest vintage clothing store *(right)*. Choose from a varied collection with the help of friendly and informed staff.

EAST MERCER ST
E REPUBLICAN ST
E HARRISON ST
SUMMIT AVE EAST
BELMONT AVE EAST
11TH AVE
12TH AVE
13TH AVE
E JOHN ST
E DENNY WAY
E DENNY WAY
BROADWAY AVENUE
E OLIVE ST
E PINE ST
E PINE ST

6 Bailey/Coy Books

A city institution as well as a Broadway favorite, this store *(see p76)* is tiny by large chain standards. Expect a gracious and knowledgeable staff, and an enviable inventory – especially if you're hunting for gay and lesbian literature.

ZEBRACLUB

7 Zebraclub

This outlet of Zebraclub's downtown store *(above)* has an equally modern collection of urban fashion from designers such as Betsey Johnson and Diane Von Furstenburg.

8 The Vajra

The name translates as "Destroyer of Ignorance", and this shop is perfect for your Tibetan Buddhist meditation supplies. Look for blockprint tapestries, scented oils, and incense. It's also a popular spot for tarot card reading *(below)*.

9 Harvard Exit/Egyptian Theaters

Broadway's two vintage movie houses *(below & p39)* showcase independent films from directors on the vanguard. The Seattle International Film Festival *(see p35)* makes liberal use of both the theaters each year.

10 Dick's

Seattle's homegrown version of a fast food hamburger joint, and unadulterated Americana to boot since 1954, this branch is a magnet for crowds on weekend nights. Quick and delicious, but not recommended for cholesterol watchers.

Pill Hill

An affectionate term for First Hill, the area almost indistinct from Capitol Hill along the same high ridge above downtown. It's thick with most of the area's hospitals and medical research facilities, hence the nickname.

Top 10 Lake Washington Ship Canal

What began in Montlake as a tiny log flume is now an 8-mile (13-km) urban waterway for sailboats, kayakers, and an impressive fleet of industrial vessels heading to sea. In 1854, pioneer Thomas Mercer recognized the need for a passage to the ocean from Seattle's two landlocked water bodies, Lake Washington and Lake Union, to replace the cumbersome transport of natural resources such as coal and timber. The Ship Canal and the Locks were completed in 1917 by the US Army Corps of Engineers. Four drawbridges cross the Canal at strategic points in Ballard, Fremont, the University District, and Montlake, at the western edge of Lake Washington.

Kayaks

If you plan on kayaking, be wary of weather changes any time of year, as winds can pick up and severely affect current and surface water conditions. Look out for larger ships that may sneak up unknowingly on smaller craft.

- *Map E2*
- *Hiram Chittenden Locks: 3015 NW 54th St; (206) 783-7059; Grounds: open 7am–9pm daily; Visitor center: open May–Sep 10am–6pm daily, Oct–Apr 10am–4pm Thu–Mon*

Top 10 Sights

1. Making the Cut
2. Bascule Bridges
3. Montlake
4. Lake Union
5. Working Waterfront
6. Christmas Ships
7. Sleepless in Seattle
8. Urban Wildlife
9. The Locks
10. Shilshole Bay

1 Making the Cut

Retired US Army Corps of Engineers general, Hiram M. Chittenden, lobbied Congress to fund the initial earth moving in 1911. Part of the Canal's construction necessitated lowering Lake Washington's water level by 9-ft (3-m).

2 Bascule Bridges

These bridges operate with counterweights and cantilevered sections that can be raised and lowered. Fremont and Ballard Bridges are the oldest, built in 1917. The former is only 30-ft (9-m) above the water line, and opens about 35 times each day *(below)*.

3 Montlake

At the base of Capitol Hill's northeastern tip, the upmarket community of Montlake abuts the Arboretum and the Ship Canal. Just across the Canal, the university's huge Husky Stadium *(above & p23)* dominates the majestic view.

Ballard
NW MARKET ST
LEARY AVE NW
GOVERNMENT WAY
15TH AVE W
NICKERSON ST
PHINNEY AVE N
AURORA AVE N
Fremont
10 9 2 2 1 7 4 8 3

4 Lake Union

A very urban lake with Seattle's downtown skyline framing its southern shore *(above)*. Seattle's maritime museum, Center for Wooden Boats *(see p37)* and South Lake Union Park at the south end are worth a visit.

8 Urban Wildlife

Although the Ship Canal is literally and figuratively far from any wilderness it still attracts diverse wildlife. Blue heron, gulls, beaver, Canada geese, and migrating salmon are among the many creatures to look for.

9 The Locks

Officially completed in 1917, the Hiram C. Chittenden Locks link the Sound and Salmon Bay at Ballard *(left)*. About 100,000 vessels pass through annually, as do salmon runs in the adjacent fish ladder – fully equipped with observation windows for visitors.

10 Shilshole Bay

The western terminus of the Ship Canal feeds into this scenic bay, home to a public marina. The waterfront boasts fine seafood restaurants, meeting spaces, and Golden Gardens *(see p47)* park.

5 Working Waterfront

Seattle's maritime industry prospers along the Ship Canal route. Tanker ships or gill netters lie in dry dock, boat dealers proliferate, and oil booms float here and there – in stark contrast to the natural ecology that struggles to survive.

6 Christmas Ships

Every December, local boaters celebrate the holiday season by venturing out during several cold evenings after decorating their boats with creative and colorful light displays.

7 Sleepless in Seattle

The idiosyncratic floating home enclaves *(below)* of northern Lake Union and Portage Bay are visible almost exclusively by boats traveling the Canal and environs. One was a focal point in the Meg Ryan and Tom Hanks romantic film, *Sleepless in Seattle* (1993).

Opening Day Events

Seattleites naturally take water and boating very seriously, but anyone can sail the waterways. The official boating season begins May 1, with a series of waterborne celebrations sponsored by the Seattle Yacht Club. Constant drawbridge openings snarl traffic for the Parade and Regatta, as the region's small ships fill the Ship Canal and adjacent lakes with revelers and those captains who may have waited all winter to sail.

The Locks have been designated a National Historic Place. They are still operated by the US Army Corps of Engineers.

TOP 10 University of Washington

Founded in November 1861, just 10 years after the creation of Washington Territory, the prestigious UW now occupies 693 hilly acres that were originally cleared for the festival grounds of Seattle's Alaska-Yukon-Pacific Exposition in 1909. Supporting a 40,000-member student body that's as eclectic as the architectural mix on campus, the institution has garnered a reputation internationally for its undergraduate and postgraduate curriculums in biomedical research, ethnomusicology, computer science, and literature. Wide open quads, cherry blossoms in spring, and landscaping provides a relaxing counterpoint to the constant buzz of advanced learning.

University campus

There's no shortage of eateries on "The Ave". For pub grub and the best microbrew in the U District, try Big Time Brewery & Alehouse (206-545-4509).

Nothing beats a meal and drinks at Agua Verde Café and Paddle Club (206-545-8570). Rent kayaks bound for Lakes Washington and Union, via the Ship Canal. Get there early for lunch or dinner to avoid the lines.

- *Map E2*
- *UW: (206) 543-9198; www.washington.edu*
- *Henry Art Gallery: (206) 543-2280; www.henryart.org* • *Meany Theater: 4001 University Way NE; (206) 543-4880*
- *Burke Museum: (206) 543-5590* • *University Book Store: 4326 University Way NE; 9am–9pm Mon–Fri, 10am–7pm Sat, noon–5pm Sun*

Top 10 Sights

1. The Hub
2. Red Square
3. Henry Art Gallery
4. Husky Stadium
5. Paul G. Allen Center for Computer Science
6. Meany Theater
7. Suzzallo Library
8. Burke Museum
9. Medicinal Herb Garden
10. University Book Store

1 The Hub

The main student union building is known as "The Hub" *(above)* due to its central position on campus. It's information central, as well as a venue for visiting performers.

2 Red Square

Named for the inlaid brick pavers underfoot, the huge Square lies between Meany Theater, Kane Hall, and the Suzzallo Library. It's also known for hosting impromptu midnight concerts by musicians seeking free expression.

University of Washington

3 Henry Art Gallery

Founded in 1927, this was the first public art gallery *(below & p36)* in Washington, which quadrupled its size in 1997 to make room for larger, adventurous, modern exhibits and collections and to enhance collaborative educational programs. It also has a bookstore and a café.

A walk around the University campus especially during spring is definitely a worthwhile experience.

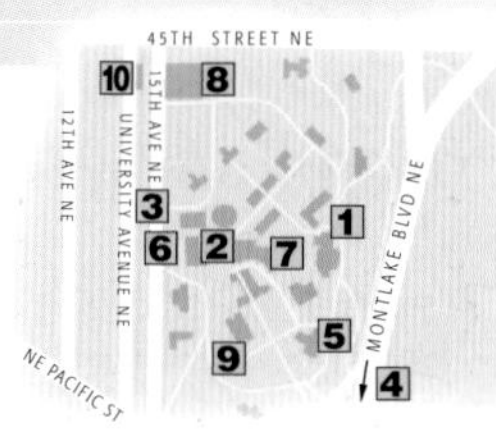

4 Husky Stadium

At the base of Capitol Hill's northeastern tip, the up-market community of Montlake abuts the Arboretum and the Ship Canal *(see pp20–21)*. Just across the Canal, the university's huge Husky Stadium, the home of the top-rated UW Huskies, dominates the view.

5 Paul G. Allen Center for Computer Science

In 2003, the University's computer sciences department moved into a $72 million facility named after one of the two founders of Microsoft.

9 Medicinal Herb Garden

Escape for a captivating spell on 2-acres of land *(below)* where several hundred species flourish and herbal scents abound. It also features a Drug Plant Garden planted in 1911.

10 University Book Store

The main branch of the bookstore rivals the best in independent and larger chain book vendors for sheer selection and informed staff.

6 Meany Theater

The shining glory of professional performance arts on campus, the theater hosts performers of all disciplines from all over the globe. It also supports the school's drama, music, dance, and experimental digital media curriculums.

7 Suzzallo Library

Once known as "the soul of the University," the library is the crowning glory of the Neo-Gothic style on campus. The astounding vaulted ceiling rises 65-ft (20-m) above the second floor reading room. It also offers classes on research and technology skills.

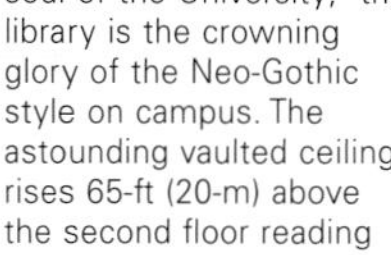

8 Burke Museum

The state's official museum *(below)* for natural and cultural history is a jewel of the campus. Its collection includes a number of Pacific Rim and Pacific Northwest coastal Native American art. The museum also organizes specialized tours and a summer discovery camp for children.

The Ave

The main commercial artery serving the U District is University Way NE, called "The Ave," which is all about youth culture. It's lined with coffee shops, music stores, clothiers, as well as bookstores that have lasted generations, and restaurants serving reasonably priced food from every culture imaginable. In 2003, in a grand effort to beautify the street, the city widened sidewalks, and enhanced law enforcement, adding some sparkle to what had been suffering neglect for years.

Woodland Park Zoo

Designed in 1909 by architect John Olmsted, this is one of the oldest zoos on the West Coast. Occupying an area of 92 acres, the landscape offers a natural habitat for nearly 300 animal species. Reflecting a naturalistic mission to advocate conservation and education while imparting the value of an ecological perspective, the animal habitats are as close to nature as possible. African mammals roam grasslands of a savanna; Asian elephants thrive in Thai-style setting; grizzly bears frolic over logs and in a stream running down a steep hill. A popular attraction for families with young children is the petting zoo, literally a hands-on activity that's fun and educational.

Main entrance gate to Woodland Park Zoo

Inside the West Gate are several places to eat in the Pavillion, where you'll find the Naturally Untamed Grill, the Rainforest Deli, Bamboo Hut, and other food counters.

You can visit Woodland Park across Hwy 99 (Aurora Avenue) from the zoo.

- *Map D1*
- *Woodland Park Zoo: 601 North 59th St; (206) 684 4800, Open mid-Mar–Apr: 9:30am–5pm daily; May–mid-Sep: 9:30am–6pm daily; mid-Sep–mid-Oct: 9:30am–5pm daily; mid-Oct– mid-Mar: 9:30am–4pm daily; Adm: Adults (13-64) $10, child (3-12) $7, toddler (0–2) free; www.zoo.org*

Top 10 Sights

1. Jaguar
2. Gorillas
3. Elephant House
4. African Savanna
5. Nocturnals
6. Birds of Prey
7. Northern Trail
8. Orangutans/Siamangs
9. Komodo Dragons
10. Plants & Pathways

1 Jaguar

The largest cat species in the Western Hemisphere found a home here in 2003 *(above)*. The habitat features a cave, a pool for his swimming preferences,and jungle-like terrain that brings the fearsome animal close enough to touch save for the glass enclosure.

2 Gorillas

In one of the most cherished spots at the zoo you can view two multi-generational gorilla families, cavorting only inches away on the other side of the glass.

3 Elephant House

View zookeepers groom and feed the Asian elephants *(below)* several times a day. There are also scheduled demonstrations of elephants performing tasks such as log stacking.

Gardeners reserve their cherished spot each year when zoo officials unload prized composted animal manure – ZooDoo.

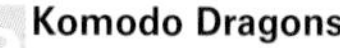

4 African Savanna

Lions, giraffes, hippos, spotted hyenas, gazelles, wild dogs, white-faced whistling duck, patas monkey, zebras, and Egyptian geese make this city-bound safari one of the largest and most exhilarating places *(below)*. Observe from an overlook dedicated to guitarist and Seattle native Jimi Hendrix.

7 Northern Trail

This is where to find the deceptively playful-looking grizzly bears *(above)*. Nearby, packs of gray or white wolves seem haunted, and the extremely threatened river otters dive underwater and re-surface with total abandon.

9 Komodo Dragons

The world's largest carnivorous lizards *(below)* can weigh as much as 500 pounds (226 kg) with a length of 9 ft (3 m), and are excellent swimmers. Not recommended for pets, but great for the imagination.

10 Plants & Pathways

Take the time to appreciate the careful consideration zoo landscapers have given to this human environment. The shrubbery *(below)* is lush and plentiful, and lends an exotic ambience to the occasion.

5 Nocturnals

Take a break from the screech and howls of outdoor wildlife for the dark and silent mysteries of nocturnal creatures. Watch boas, pythons, vampire bats, tomato frogs, blue-tongued skinks, and much more.

6 Birds of Prey

Watch falconers send regal winged predators out and back by the Raptor Center. Perched on fence posts, owls *(right)* and red-tailed hawks may reside calmly in full panoramic view.

8 Orangutans/ Siamangs

With intelligence that approaches our own, orangutans are still hilarious to observe. Also view siamangs, native to the island of Sumatra and the Malay Peninsula.

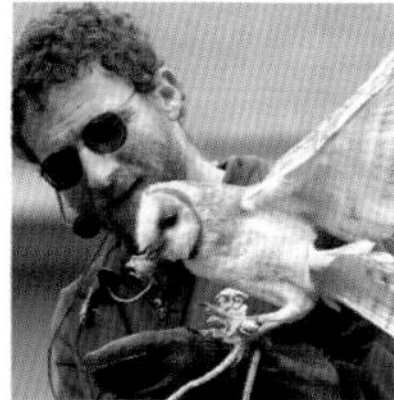

Zoo Summer Concerts

The zoo departs from its main agenda every summer with one of Seattle's musical highlights. Residents from the surrounding neighborhood and all over town meet on the North Meadow in the late afternoons and early evenings for a picnic dinner, and take in entertainment from some of the best known musicians worldwide. In keeping with the zoo's family theme, children under 12 are admitted free.

Look out for the iridescent tail feathers of resident peacocks who wander the walkways and surprise onlookers.

TOP 10 Discovery Park

Occupying the northwestern edge of the Magnolia headland north of Elliott Bay, Discovery Park is Seattle's largest and most varied in-city escape. Even though the US Army's Fort Lawton sold surplus base territory to the city, Army Reserves still use a portion of the park for training and officers' quarters. At 534 acres, the park consists of densely wooded rainforests crisscrossed with trails, high bluffs of eroding sand at the edge of a huge meadow, and 2 miles (3 km) of driftwood laden beaches on Puget Sound, providing a real sense of wildness.

A beach at Discovery Park

Plan an itinerary in advance based on the amount of time you have to spare. There are no concessions in the park, so bring snacks or a picnic lunch.

- *Map A2*
- *Discovery Park: 3801 W Government Way; (206) 386-4236, 4am–11:30pm daily; Visitors' center; 8:30am–5pm Tue–Sun; www.discoverypark.org*
- *Daybreak Star Indian Cultural Center: (206) 285-4425*

Top 10 Sights

1. Bluff Trail
2. Military Residences
3. Daybreak Star Indian Cultural Center
4. West Point Lighthouse
5. Beach Walks at Low Tide
6. Loop Trail
7. Eagle Watching
8. Playgrounds
9. West Point Treatment Plant
10. Go Fly a Kite

1 Bluff Trail

The trail leads from the South Gate along a meadow's edge to the majestic overlook with breathtaking views of the Olympic Mountains and Puget Sound.

2 Military Residences

The park is dotted with clusters of abandoned and still-in-use army base housing, listed on the National Register of Historic Places. Most are off limits to visitors, but you can get a closer look at them near the former parade grounds.

3 Daybreak Star Indian Cultural Center

Operated by the United Indians of All Tribes Foundation, the center houses a collection of Native American art. There's an arts and crafts gallery, traditional salmon bakes, and an annual summer pow wow celebration *(below)* on the grounds of Discovery Park.

4 West Point Lighthouse

As picturesque as can be, the lighthouse *(below)* shines light through the fog from its perch on a narrow spit of land jutting out into the water. Feel free to stroll up to and around the automated sentinel, even though it's not open for touring.

Stay off the sandy, constantly eroding bluffs. Rangers periodically relocate the Bluff Trail to prevent accidents.

5 Beach Walks at Low Tide

Seattleites escaping the hustle and bustle of the city come to walk along the waterfront parks around the Sound. The beach at Discovery Park is a preferred spot for those in the know.

8 Playgrounds

For an outing with children, head for the small playground behind park headquarters at the East entrance. Or, ask for one of only five parking passes available for families with young children so you can drive directly down to the alluring shore of Discovery Park.

10 Go Fly a Kite

The hilly field between the main bluffs and a radar ball behind barbed wire makes for some of the best kite flying *(above)* in town, as updrafts from the sea seem almost constant throughout the year.

6 Loop Trail

Stroll along the trail that brings you through the varied terrain of Discovery Park. Explore the easy route to find overgrown rainforest ravines, flowering meadowlands, creeks, thickets, streams, sand dunes, and blackberry brambles galore.

9 West Point Treatment Plant

An extraordinary reminder of the city outside, this facility is so exquisitely landscaped to be almost invisible from hiking trails. This ultra-modern wastewater treatment plant is as environmentally conscious as technology allows.

7 Eagle Watching

Occasionally, bald eagles *(right)* nest in the highest treetops in Discovery Park, home to more than 250 species of birds and other wildlife. You may find park volunteers surrounded by eager bird-watchers with binoculars. Chances are, they have sighted a nest.

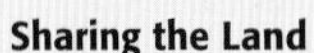

Sharing the Land

In many ways, land use at Discovery Park represents the harmonious balance between natural conservation and urban development, and a co-existence of US military and Native American tribes. In 1970, a group of protesters led by activist Bernie Whitebear staged an invasion and occupation of the still active military base, in part to establish a cultural land foundation for urban Indians. After an exhausting three months for both sides, and many arrests, Whitebear's group acquired a 99-year lease for 20 acres of parkland.

Following pages **West Point Lighthouse at Discovery Park**

Left **European settlers, West Seattle** Right **Klondike Gold Rush National Historical Park**

Top 10 Moments in History

1 Native American Roots
Archaeological records date the first inhabitants of the Seattle region to 11,000-12,000 years ago. Tribes included the Suquamish, Duwamish, Nisqually, Snoqualmie, and Muckleshoot, who, despite their harsh environment, evolved into complex societies that traded with other tribes.

2 Denny Party
In 1851, Chief Sealth of the Duwamish Tribe greeted Arthur A. Denny and his group of European settlers at West Seattle's Alki Point *(see p97)*. Subsequently, Denny served as a delegate to the Monticello convention, which gave rise to the states of Oregon and Washington.

Arthur A. Denny

3 Northern Pacific Railroad
Seattle's neighbor, Tacoma, was the original terminus of 1873's Northern Pacific Railroad, linking the region to the rest of the country. By 1893, another transcontinental railroad, the Great Northern Railway, extended into Seattle, eventually supplanting Tacoma as the Puget Sound region's main rail depot.

4 Lumber Mills
When timber baron Frederick Weyerhaeuser purchased nearly a million acres of railroad land in 1900, Seattle's mushrooming logging industry turned a corner for even more rapid growth and exploitation of natural resources. Until then, entrepreneurs such as Henry Yesler ruled the wharf, and erected the pioneer town out of lumber from ancient old growth forests.

5 Great Fire of 1889
Natural resources created a boomtown whose rapid growth drew more than 1,000 new residents every month. Seattleites learned the impermanence of wooden structures in 1889, after a catastrophic fire destroyed much of the downtown area.

6 Klondike Gold Rush
The Alaska Gold Rush *(see p15)* officially kicked off in 1897 after a gold-filled steamship docked at Seattle's waterfront. As the last gas for prospectors and suppliers bound for the gold fields, this city prospered as never before.

7 Boeing's Beginnings
Recognizing the need for airplanes as the United States entered World War I in 1917, William E. Boeing hired pilot Herb Munter to design a seaplane for the Navy. The rest of the giant Boeing Corporation's success is history.

Devastation after the 2001 earthquake

8 Rise of Microsoft

In 1975, Harvard dropout Bill Gates and his high school friend Paul Allen founded Microsoft. From the suburb of Redmond, they launched a personal computer revolution and have never looked back. Today, Microsoft's Windows operating system is the dominant computer platform, and the company employs more than 50,000 people worldwide.

9 Nisqually Earthquake

If Seattle is a boom and bust town, it certainly felt the boom in a magnitude-6.8 earthquake on the morning of February 28, 2001 *(see p15)*. Workers escaped their offices, if they could, to see the earth rolling, pavements cracking, and cars violently swaying. The region suffered more than $1 billion in damages.

10 Green River Killer Caught

The Seattle area lived under a dark shadow of brutal serial killings as dozens of women became victims of the Green River Killer. Twenty years of intense investigation led to the capture of Gary Ridgeway in 2001. He was convicted in 2003.

Top 10 Famous Seattleites

1 Chief Sealth (1786–1866)
Seattle draws its name from the Duwamish leader.

2 John Nordstrom (1871–1963)
Originally a shoe seller, the Nordstrom family empire is now a chain of upscale department stores.

3 Eddie Bauer (1899–1986)
The inventor of the goose-down parka opened his first store of clothes and sporting goods in Seattle.

4 Bruce Lee (1940–1973)
This Kung-Fu legend and movie star lived in Seattle.

5 Jimi Hendrix (1942–1970)
A self-taught and innovative electric guitarist, Hendrix's original compositions continue to influence today's music.

6 Ted Bundy (1946–1989)
The serial killer of the 1980s admitted to 30 murders and was executed in 1989.

7 Howard Schultz (b. 1953)
Schultz turned a few local coffee stores into the global Starbucks Empire worth billions of dollars.

8 Bill Gates (b. 1955)
Co-founder of Microsoft and one of the world's richest men, he continues to run the company today.

9 Jeff Bezos (b. 1964)
This Internet billionaire founded giant web retailer Amazon.com in 1995.

10 Gary Locke (b. 1949)
The first Asian-American governor in the US, Locke was elected in 1997.

Left **EMP** Center **Pioneer Building** Right **Metro Bus Tunnel**

Top 10 Architectural Highlights

1 Space Needle

Seattle's modern architectural identity began with the Space Needle *(see p10)*, designed by John Graham and Company, for the 1962 World's Fair. The three pairs of beams supporting the spire lie buried 30-ft (8-m) underground, and have secured the 605-ft (185-m) Needle during several earthquakes and gale-force windstorms. *Map H2*

2 Experience Music Project

Designed by renowned Post-Modern architect, Frank Gehry, this technicolor facility *(see p10)* resembles a smashed guitar, in homage to the incendiary finales of Jimi Hendrix's early career. Paul Allen's provocative project emphasizes Seattle's role at the artistic and musical vanguard. *Map H2 • 325 5th Ave N*

3 Koolhaas Library

Award-winning Dutch architect Rem Koolhaas designed the $196.4 million insulated glass and steel structure to replace Seattle's vintage-1960 Central Library. The unusual oblique structure and glass flooring have been controversial, but defenders of the building insist that once inside, people will love it. *See p64. Map K5 • 1000 4th Ave*

Koolhaas Library

4 Columbia Tower

This 76-story skyscraper rises high above any other Seattle structure. Completed in 1985, from a design by Chester Lindsey Architects, it holds the US record for most stories in any building west of the Mississippi River. Three of the 46 elevators bring visitors to the posh private club at the top. It offers stunning views of Elliott Bay, the Olympic Peninsula, Mount Rainier, and the Cascade Mountains. *Map K5 • 701 5th Ave • (206) 386-5151 • 8:30–4:30 Mon–Fri • Adm for observation deck*

5 Monorail

One of the city's favorite attractions is the Monorail, an exciting 90-second ride *(see pp11 & 64)* designed by Alweg Rapid Transit Systems. Each year, 2.5 million passengers board its original 1962 cars to get a taste of what designers imagined would be the mass transit model of the future. Unfortunately, a train collision in 2005 has closed down the monorail for the time being and plans to extend the system for mass transit have been put on hold. *Map H2 • 370 Thomas St • (206) 448-3481*

Monorail replacement buses operate between Seattle Center and Westlake Center: Mon–Fri 7am–7pm, Sat–Sun 9am–9pm

6 Rainier Tower

Designed by renowned Japanese architect Minoru Yamasaki in 1977, this unique 40-story structure resembles an upside-down skyscraper, as its main tower rises from a relatively narrow 11-story pedestal. Rainier Square *(see p53)*, an upscale underground shopping mall, occupies much of its ground level. ✎ *Map K4 • 1333 5th Ave*

Brass elevator doors of the 1914 Smith Tower

7 Seattle Tower

This charming Art Deco building was designed by architects Albertson, Wilson & Richardson in 1929. The façade's tan brick and multiple shades of granite set it apart from its steel and glass neighbors. Vertical accents make its 27 stories appear even taller, and the lobby's ornate bronze and marble detail is capped by a fanciful ceiling bas-relief depicting local flora and fauna. ✎ *Map K4 • 1218 3rd Ave*

8 Smith Tower

Typewriter tycoon L.C. Smith erected Seattle's first skyscraper *(see p14)* in 1914. The white terra-cotta building has brass hand-operated elevators that take visitors to the Chinese Room at the 35th level, with its antique carvings and inlaid porcelain ceiling, and an observation deck. ✎ *Map K5 • 506 2nd Ave • Adm for observation deck • www. smithtower.com*

9 Pioneer Building

This striking 1892 building of red brick and terra-cotta, designed by Elmer H. Fisher, boasts a National Historic Landmark status. During the Gold Rush years, 48 mining outfits maintained offices here, and it became headquarters for a prosperous speakeasy during Prohibition. Bill Spiedel's Underground Tour *(see p14)* starts here. ✎ *Map K5 • 608 1st Ave*

10 Downtown Seattle Transit Tunnel (DSTT)

From the Washington State Convention Center to the International District, this tunnel was designed to carry riders aboard buses that switch from diesel to electric energy while underground. All tunnel stations are within the Ride Free Zone *(see p65)*. In 2005 work began to convert the tunnel for light rail as well as bus use. During the two-year project all tunnel bus routes will operate on surface street routes. ✎ *Map K3*

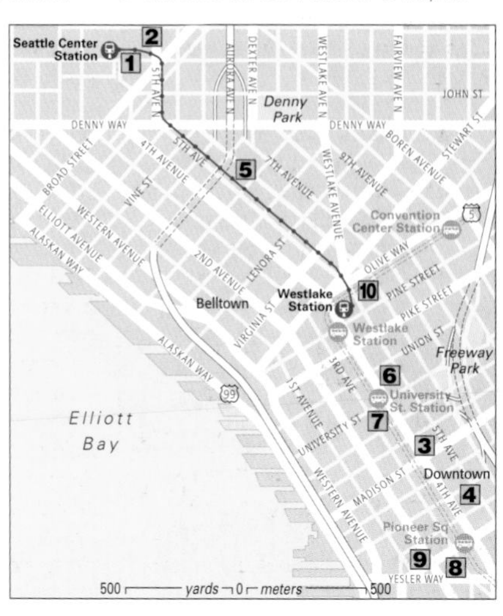

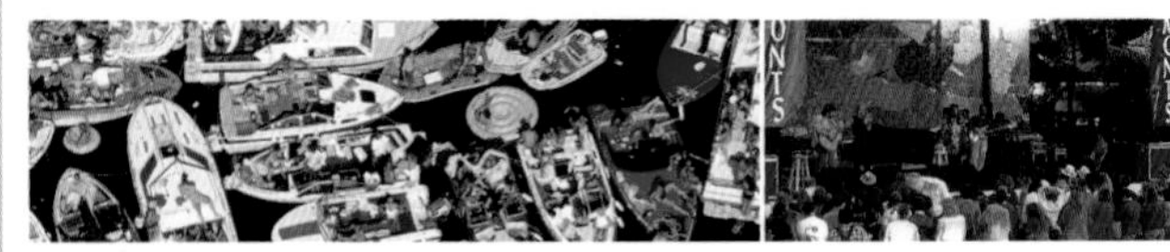

Left **Seafair** Right **Bumbershoot**

TOP 10 Festivals & Parades

1 Seafair

A parade along 4th Avenue in early July kicks off Seafair, a celebration of maritime and aviation history highlighted by the aerodynamic "derring-do" of the Navy's Blue Angels F/A-18 fighter pilots, an All Nations Pow Wow at Daybreak Cultural Center, hydroplane races on Lake Washington, and battleships open to the public on the waterfront.

Crowds watching the Blue Angels, Seafair

2 Bumbershoot

Performers from all over the world converge for this Labor Day weekend festival *(see p11)* that transforms Seattle Center into the arts capital of the Pacific NW. Its three days are packed with concerts, intimate theater productions, independent film presentations, and literary arts.

3 Seattle Pride March

The Seattle Pride March *(see p72)* runs from Westlake Park to Seattle Center. Sponsored by the gay, lesbian, bisexual, and transgender community, it attracts huge crowds from every orientation. Expect outrageous floats, dancing, and the popular "Dykes on Bikes", a motorcycle outfit whose members freely show what they have beneath the leather.

4 University District Street Fair

Dating from 1970, Seattle's first street fair stretches over ten blocks of "The Ave" and its side-streets in May. Innumerable crafts booths, food vendors, and local rock music performances attract families from all over town.

5 Fremont Fair Solstice Parade

All floats at this innovative parade must be entirely human powered, stimulating the imaginations of Fremont's anarchic arts community. Crews propel samba bands, dancers, and rock quartets using battery-operated amplifiers. It's held on or near the summer solstice (June 21).

6 Seattle Maritime Festival

Aficionados of tugboats and ships flock to this May festival. It makes for a free, fun, and family-friendly way to learn how the working waterfront has become a major factor in Seattle's economy and culture. The fair centers around the Bell Street Pier, which is adjacent to the Odyssey Maritime Discovery Center *(see p13 & 37)*. An exciting and humorous highlight is the tugboat race on Elliott Bay.

For more information on Seattle Pride March, held in late June each year, visit www.seattlepride.org

7 Northwest Folklife Festival

A free May celebration of the Pacific NW's ethnic music, dance, and arts and crafts, Folklife is a magnet for all the old (and new) hippies in the region. Given the diversity of Seattle's Pacific Rim population, it's virtually a festival of and for the world.

Rainbow Lady, Folklife Festival

8 Seattle International Film Festival (SIFF)

One of the most respected and comprehensive film festivals in the US, the SIFF screens more than 300 new works from at least 50 countries during May and June. Even midnight showings of cult films sell out, and notable directors attend many premier screenings.

9 Earshot Jazz Festival

The shoestring staff at the non-profit Earshot Jazz held between October and November present a well-respected event. The festivals have consistently showcased successful as well as struggling jazz artists, enriching and enlightening the Seattle community at large. Well-known performers have included Bill Frisell and John McLaughlin.

10 Seattle Improvised Music Festival (SIMF)

The largest and longest running music festival of its kind anywhere, SIMF is dedicated to the esoteric art of spontaneous composition. Local performers join eclectic international musicians to improvise sets that defy category, but always impress. After 19 thrilling annual productions, the ever-popular February festival draws larger audiences each year.

Top 10 Festal Cultural Events

1 Tet Festival
A colorful beginning in late January marks the Vietnamese Lunar New Year.

2 Festival Sundiata
Seattle's celebration of the West African Mansa of the Mali Empire, in mid-February, represents African and African American cultural traditions.

3 Irish Week Festival
Music and dance events comprise two days of authentic Irish culture in mid-March.

4 Seattle Cherry Blossom & Japanese Cultural Festival
Dance, music, martial arts, and tea ceremonies are the highlights of this mid-April fair.

5 Pagdiriwang Philippine Festival
Philippine independence is celebrated in mid-June with colorful costumes, dance, film, drama, and culinary arts.

6 BrasilFest
Expect infectious rhythms, joyful dance, and spicy flavors to celebrate this Brazilian Folklore Day in late August.

7 TibetFest
This late-August festival preserves Tibet's rituals and traditions while incorporating cultural elements of its neighboring countries.

8 Dia de Muertos
Pay tribute to your ancestors Latin American-style with altars, artwork, food, and music in October.

9 Italian Festival
This early-October festival is all about fun and food.

10 Hmong New Year
November marks the end of harvest, a time for relaxing, and preparing special foods.

Fremont Fair Solstice Parade has a scenic location along the Ship Canal. Visit www.fremontfair.com for more information.

Left **Seattle Art Museum** Center **Frye Art Museum** Right **Henry Art Gallery**

TOP 10 Museums

1 Seattle Art Museum

Jonathan Borofsky's 48-ft (15-m) tall, black metal *Hammering Man* stands at the entrance of Seattle's largest art museum *(see p63)*. SAM's permanent collection of approximately 23,000 objects includes European, Asian, African, and Northwest Coast Native American works. *Map J4 • 100 University St • (206) 654-3100 • Closed for refurbishment until spring 2007 • Adm (free 1st Thu of month) • www.seattleartmuseum.org*

Hammering Man

2 Seattle Asian Art Museum

The historic 1933 Art-Moderne structure in Volunteer Park houses Seattle Art Museum's Asian art collection, primarily works from China, Japan, and Korea. Under renovation until 2010. *Map E4 • 1400 E Prospect St • (206) 654-3100 • Adm*

3 Frye Art Museum

Wealthy industrialists Emma and Charles Frye's extensive collection of 19th–20th century representational art is on view at this elegant gallery. Exhibits include works by American masters such as Mary Cassatt, Thomas Eakins, Winslow Homer, John Singer Sargent, and Andrew Wyeth. *Map L4 • 704 Terry Ave • Open 10am–5pm Tue–Wed & Fri–Sat, 10am–8pm Thu, noon–5pm Sun • Adm • www.fryeart.org*

Seattle Asian Art Museum

4 Museum of History & Industry

This is a gem for anyone interested in the region's work and workers over the last 150 years. Key features include 1.5 million online photographs, a rich catalog of oral histories, and educational programs. *Map F3 • 2700 24th Ave E • (206) 324-1126 • Open 10am–5pm daily, 10am–8pm 1st Thu of month • Adm (free 1st Thu of month)*

5 Henry Art Gallery

This modern art museum *(see p23)* at UW presents work by cutting-edge artists. It also offers imaginative programs and exhibits, and promotes experimental art by encouraging dialogue on contemporary culture, politics, and aesthetics. *Map E2 • NE 41st St & 15th Ave NE • (206) 543-2280 • Open 11am–5pm Tue–Wed & Fri–Sun, 11am–8pm Thu • Adm (free Thu)*

6 Burke Museum

Founded in 1885, the Burke is a natural history buff's dream. View dinosaur and dragonfly fossils, hand-carved Native-American cedar canoes, and gems and minerals. ⊛ *Map E2 • NE 45 St & 17th Ave NE • (206) 543-5590 • Open 10am–5pm daily • Adm (free 1st Thu of month)*

7 Odyssey Maritime Discovery Center

One of Seattle's lesser known attractions opened in 1998. The center *(see p13)* offers a perfect rainy day escape for families with children, as hands-on exhibits give kids a real feel of a maritime city. Captain a ferry, container ship, or a tugboat, or learn about the fishing industry.

8 Museum of Flight

The museum *(see p41)* at Boeing Field provides insightful programs and great aerospace artifacts. Walk through a model of the Space Shuttle, tour the first Air Force One, designed for President Kennedy, climb into the cockpit of a mint-condition SR-71 Blackbird or F/A-18 Hornet fighter jet, or come see the latest addition, a Concorde. ⊛ *Map P2 • 9404 E Marginal Way S • Adm*

9 Center for Wooden Boats

CWB advocates the history and craftsmanship of boats by presenting maritime heritage activities and classes. During their annual July festival, you can tour relic sloops and tugs. For an in-city adventure, try sailing one of the historic boats. ⊛ *Map D4 • 1010 Valley St • (206) 382-2628*

10 Wing Luke Asian Museum

Named for a dynamic civic leader who lobbied for Asian-American rights, this museum fulfills Wing's dream to showcase the culture and history of Asian immigrants. Artifacts include Chinese lanterns and a 50-ft (15-m) dragon boat. ⊛ *Map L6 • 407 7th Ave S • (206) 623-5124 • Adm*

Top 10 Northwest Artists

1 Jacob Lawrence (1917–2000)

Lawrence established a national reputation as a painter and activist.

2 Mark Tobey (1890–1976)

A 1953 *Life* magazine featured Tobey as one of the four "Mystic Painters of the Pacific Northwest." He was a major influence on Jackson Pollock.

3 George Tsutakawa (1910–1997)

He gained international fame as a painter, sculptor, and fountain maker.

4 Morris Graves (1910–2001)

This Northwest painter continues to inspire Seattle artists.

5 Paul Horiuchi (1906–1999)

His heavily textured, abstract Expressionist collage painting utilized Zen philosophy to create mysterious works.

6 Guy Anderson (1906–1998)

Part of the 1953 *Life* feature, Anderson led an eccentric but influential life as a painter.

7 Kenneth Callahan (1905–1986)

Another artist in the *Life* feature, he was once a curator at Seattle Art Museum.

8 Tony Angell (b. 1940)

A naturalistic painter, sculptor, and writer.

9 Dale Chihuly (b. 1941)

Chihuly's handblown decorative glass art has popularized the medium.

10 Clayton James (b. 1918)

James painted landscapes, made furniture, and sculpted in multiple media.

Left **Benaroya Hall** Center **Moore Theater sign** Right **Bagley Wright Theatre**

TOP 10 Performing Arts Venues

1 Benaroya Hall

This bastion of culture is the city's first venue designed exclusively for music performances. It is also home to the Seattle Symphony. The 2,500-seat Mark Taper auditorium is known for its superior acoustics. Another 540-seat hall is used for smaller concerts. *Map K4 • 200 University St • (206) 215-4747 • www.seattlesymphony.org*

2 McCaw Hall

In 2003 the original opera house underwent a massive transformation to become McCaw Hall *(see p10)*. Built for no less than $127 million, this plush 2,900-seat auditorium with state-of-the-art acoustics and excellent amenities is home to the Seattle Opera and Pacific Northwest Ballet. *Map H1*

3 KeyArena

The largest indoor venue *(see p11)* in Seattle Center is home to the city's professional men's and women's basketball teams, Seattle Supersonics and Seattle Storm, and the Thunderbirds hockey team. Concerts are also held here. *Map G2*

KeyArena

4 Paramount Theater

One of the most treasured theaters in town, the faithfully restored Paramount dates from 1928 and exudes the charm of the popular Beaux Arts style of grand movie palaces of its period. Today, it presents Broadway shows, jazz and rock concerts, and dance performances. *Map K3 • 911 Pine St • (206) 467-5510 • www.theparamount.com*

5 Moore Theater

Built in 1907, the grand lobby and halls of Seattle's oldest theater flow with mosaic, stained glass, and woodcarvings. In 1974, it was placed on the National Register of Historic Places. It also serves as a base for new rock bands. *Map J4 • 1932 2nd Ave • (206) 467-5510 • www.themoore.com*

6 5th Avenue Theatre

Opening in 1926 as a vaudeville venue, 5th Avenue's ornate imperial Chinese design was inspired by Beijing's Forbidden City. It is Seattle's premier home for nationally touring musical theater. *Map K4 • 1308 5th Ave • (206) 625-1418 • www.5thavenuetheatre.org*

7 Bagley Wright Theatre

The large green building at the Seattle Center belongs to the non-profit Seattle Repertory Theatre. The Bagley Wright Hall *(see p11)* is the flagship of the company's three performance

Broadway Performance Hall

venues. The Rep won the 1990s Tony Award for Outstanding Regional Theater, confirming its reputation for producing classic and contemporary plays of high literary standards. *Map H1• 155 Mercer St • (877) 900-9285*

8 ACT Theatre/ Kreielsheimer Place

Housed in the beautifully refurbished Kreielsheimer Place (formerly Eagles Auditorium), the long-running A Contemporary Theatre showcases contemporary playwrights. Inside, the cultural center contains four performance spaces, ACT's administrative offices, rehearsal spaces, and scene and costume shops. *Map K4 • 700 Union St • (206) 292-7676 • www.acttheatre.org*

9 Broadway Performance Hall

Victor Steinbrueck, who helped preserve Pike Place Market *(see pp8–9)*, was also instrumental in saving this auditorium *(see p18)* from the wrecking ball. Its repertoire includes film festivals, music and dance recitals, and off-the-wall theater. *Map L3*

10 Sky Church

EMP's performance venue *(see p10)* is a 85-ft (26-m) high room, the ultimate facility for a band looking to use 48,000 watts of surround-sound amplification, exceptional computer-controlled light systems, and the world's largest indoor video screen. *Map H2 • 325 5th Ave N • (877) 367-5483 • www.emplive.com*

Top 10 Best Cinemas

1 Egyptian

With its kitschy decor the theater housed the SIFF in the 1980s. *Map L3 • 805 E Pine St • (206) 781-5755*

2 Harvard Exit

Seattle's first art movie house. *Map L2 • 807 E Roy St • (206) 781-5755*

3 NW Film Forum

Has an independent cinema and studio for incubating new work. *Map M3 • 1515 12th Ave E • (206) 329-2629*

4 Cinerama

Paul Allen financed the restoration of this 808-seat movie house. *Map J3 • 2100 4th Ave • (206) 441-3080*

5 Fremont Outdoor Cinema (Summers)

Favorite for cult and classic movies. *Map D2 • N 35th & Phinney Ave N • (206) 634-2150*

6 Grand Illusion

They show the best of independent and avant-garde films. *Map E2 • 1403 NE 50th St • (206) 523-3935*

7 Rendezvous Cafe/ Jewel Box

This Belltown bar's back room seats only a few diehard fans of independent film. *Map J3 • (206) 441-5823 • only Wed*

8 Majestic Bay

Ballard's vintage theater offers modern luxuries. *Map B1 • 2044 NW Market St • (206) 781-2229*

9 Neptune

Built in 1921 with a nautical motif and movie-palace grandeur. *Map E2 • 1303 NE 45th St • (206) 781-5755*

10 Varsity

The Varsity has thrived since it opened in 1940. *Map E2 • 4329 University Way NE • (206) 781-5755*

Left **Children's Museum** Center **Children's Festival** Right **Northwest Puppet Theater**

Top 10 Children's Attractions

1 Children's Museum

In the heart of Seattle Center, this museum contains imaginative galleries and hands-on studio spaces that endlessly stimulate children's imaginations. The walk-through Global Village reveals lifestyles of Japan and Ghana, and a wonderful stage invites young performers to dress up and act out scripts provided by the museum. *Map H2 • 305 Harrison St • (260) 441-1768 • Adm • www.thechildrensmuseum.org*

2 International Fountain

During any festival and all through summer, the fountain draws hundreds of frolicking children. Weather permitting, kids strip down and dodge dozens of majestic arcs of water projecting out and up from the spikey spherical base, all in time to music. *Map H2 • 205 Harrison St • (206) 684-7200 • 11am–8pm*

International Fountain

3 Kid's Bookstores

Seattle's many venues and activities designed for children include excellent bookstores with envious inventories. Stock your library with books from All for Kids and Secret Garden. *All for Kids: Map F1; 2900 NE Blakely St; (206) 526-2768 • Secret Garden: Map B1; 2214 NW Market St; (206) 789-5006*

4 Toystores

The city's most popular local toy stores have a loyal following because their toys spur children's imaginations without sparing the fun. Browse the jam-packed aisles at Top Ten Toys and Magic Mouse. *Top Ten Toys: Map P2; 104 N 85th St; (206) 782-0098 • Magic Mouse: Map K5; 603 1st Ave; (206) 682-8097*

5 Seattle International Children's Festival

Every May, Seattle Center entertains the community with talent from around the world. More than 100 productions include music, drama, puppetry, and circus arts. *Map H2 • 305 Harrison St • (206) 684-7346 • Adm*

6 Northwest Puppet Theater

Founded by the dedicated Carter Family Marionettes in 1986, this puppet center offers a museum, archive and library, and over 250 annual performances. The troupe tours and also sponsors educational outreach programs worldwide. *Map P2 • 9123 15th Ave NE • (206) 523-2579 • www.nwpuppet.org*

Fun Forest amusement park

7 Fun Forest

Another remnant of the World's Fair, this tiny amusement park has loud carnival rides and games. Kids love the bumper cars and the small but exciting roller coaster. The entertainment pavilion offers laser tag, mini-golf, and a video arcade. *Map H2 • 305 Harrison St • (206) 728-1585 • Open daily*

8 Museum of Flight

Many children wish to fly, or fly off the handle. Either way, one way to encourage the former and stifle the latter is to take them to this museum *(see p37)*. It also provides insightful outreach programs for school groups, families, and teachers.

9 Ride the Ducks

If you can't decide between a tour by land or sea, these amphibious vehicles from World War II make for an offbeat excursion around the waters of Seattle. Areas include downtown, the Pike Place Market, Pioneer Square, Fremont, and Lake Union's houseboats. *Map H2 • 516 Broad St • (800) 817-1116*

10 Tillicum Village

Blake Island, across the bay from the waterfront, contains a rainforest park and a fabricated Northwest Coastal Native American Village. A four-hour adventure includes the cruise, a traditional buffet, and time to stroll beaches and forested trails. *Map B5 • 2992 SW Avalon Way • (206) 933-8600*

Top 10 Hotels with Swimming Pools

1 Warwick Hotel

This Belltown hotel's many 24-hour extras and the pool make it even more family-friendly. *(see p118)*

2 Inn at Harbor Steps

This upscale inn features large, well-appointed rooms in the heart of the city. The pool, gym, and sauna are the icing on the cake. *(see p115)*

3 Marriott Courtyard

Relax in the hot tub while the kids frolic in the indoor pool. *Map D4 • 925 Westlake Ave N • (206) 213-0100*

4 Sheraton

Parents may prefer idle moments in the wine bar called the Gallery, but the hotel also has a heated indoor pool for all ages. *(see p114)*

5 Westin

The indoor pool is an all-weather plus. *(see p114)*

6 University Inn

Families will appreciate the inn's 100-percent non-smoking rule and free breakfast. *(see p116)*

7 Travelodge Space Needle

Amenities are few, but there is a children's play area, free breakfast, and an outdoor pool. *(see p118)*

8 Fairmont Olympic

The indoor pool is just one of many amenities for those with deep pockets. *(see p114)*

9 Holiday Inn Express

Its proximity to Fun Forest and the highway has its obvious conveniences. *(see p118)*

10 Silver Cloud Inn

Take advantage of this inn's pool, complimentary breakfasts, and shuttles to downtown. *(see p116)*

Left **Visitors at Greenlake** Right **Boaters on Greenlake**

TOP 10 Seattle Pastimes

1 Coffee Town

Seattle's signature beverage comes in myriad forms. The rampant availability of whole bean, latte, espresso, and basic drip created a coffee craze even before Starbucks went global. Though Seattelites love their streetside espresso carts and neighborhood cafés, the city is also home to Starbucks and its major competitors, Tully's and Seattle's Best Coffee.

Cold coffee

2 Gardening

Gardeners take advantage of the weather to grow astounding varieties of plants and trees that thrive in the mist and drizzle. Despite the short growing season, there's enough sunshine to keep urban pea patches and botanical gardens as thick and green as the rainforests are tall.

3 Kites at GasWorks Park

A favorite gathering spot is a hill overlooking Lake Union at GasWorks Park *(see p46)*. The wind patterns at this point attract kite flyers of all ages.

4 Public Art

Public art seems to grow like weeds, particularly in Fremont *(see pp81–83)*. Even bus tours cruise by the incongruous collection here — dinosaur topiaries, a Volkswagen-crushing troll under a highway, and a statue of Lenin, from the former Soviet Union. Other installations include *Waiting for the Interurban*, depicting bored commuters.

5 Code Warriors

Microsoft, its supporting vendors, and upstart competitors still employ thousands of computer programmers and developers. Writing the killer application inspires many an entrepreneur. The laptop user at the café table next to yours may well be the next software mogul.

6 Greenlake Jogs

Greenlake *(see p46)* attracts health- and nature-conscious visitors from around the city. A verdant setting and wide 2.8-mile (4.5-km) path encircling the lake attracts walkers, runners, bikers, and babystroller-pushing parents come rain or shine.

Kite flying at GasWorks Park

7 Readings & Lectures

Many authors make their home here, and historical fiction, music biography, and science fiction are just a few popular genres that have taken root. Pioneer Square's Elliott Bay Book Company *(see p10)* sponsors one of the region's most treasured reading and lecture series.

8 Historic Preservation

Seattle maintains a vital link to its past through architecture, due to the remarkable success of its preservationists. Pike Place Market *(see pp8–9)* is one shining example, and several downtown theaters and 19th-century structures in Pioneer Square *(see pp14–15)* have achieved landmark status. Seattle neighborhoods reveal several restored Craftsman-style homes.

9 Boating

An aerial view of Seattle reveals that this town practically floats in a vast watershed. Natural and man-made canals, rivers, lakes, and estuaries abound. Pleasure boats and commercial ships of all kinds ply the waterways of one of the busiest and most picturesque maritime communities in the United States.

10 Civil Unrest

When the WTO met in Seattle in 1999, thousands of demonstrators turned the city upside down. But that was only the most recent chapter in a long history of civil disobedience. In the early 20th century, the International Workers of the World unionized logging and mining industries. Violent riots erupted in 1916 in Everett and in 1919 in Centralia, cities to the north and south of Seattle.

Top 10 Cafés

1 B&O Espresso

A destination for coffee, complete meals, and rich desserts piled high. *(see p75)*

2 Bauhaus Books & Café

(see p75)

3 Caffé Lladro

This local chain captures the basic espresso requirements: consistent pours and loyal clientele. *Map E4 • 435 15th E • (206) 267-0551*

4 Zeitgeist

They make exceptional espresso and also sponsor art shows. *Map K6 • 171 S Jackson • (206) 583-0497*

5 Elliott Bay Books & Café

(see p14)

6 Fremont Coffee Company

You'll see denizens using Wifi technology with their laptops. The coffee is superb. *Map E4 • 459 N 36th • (206) 632-3633*

7 Lighthouse Roasters

They make rich drinks from freshly roasted coffee beans. *Map D2 • 400 N 43rd • (206) 634-3140*

8 Allegro Espresso Bar

Keeps students, professors, and locals stoked on caffeine brewed to perfection. *Map L3 • 4214 University Way • (206) 633-3030*

9 Herkimer Coffee

A tastefully designed café in the quiet Greenwood neighborhood has a faithful following seven days a week. *Map P2 • 7320 Greenwood N • (206) 784-0202*

10 Tea House Kuan Yin

Offers fine teas and an ambience that's more Zen than zippy. *Map D2 • 1911 N 45th • (206) 632-2055*

Left **Sea kayaks, Lake Union** Right **A cyclist on Alki Beach**

TOP 10 Getting Physical

1 Climbing Rock Walls

The most popular indoor location for rock climbers is Recreational Equipment Incorporated (REI–*see p45*), which has a huge practice wall in the atrium of their flagship store on Eastlake Avenue. Stone Gardens also offers classes and practice walls for members and walk-ins. *Stone Gardens: Map B1 • 2839 NW Market • (206) 781-9828 • Adult $14; student $13; under 18 $9; rental equipment extra*

2 Kayaking

Lake Union is the most convenient point, being so close to downtown and its Ship Canal links to Lake Washington and Shilshole. When there's no wind, the currents are barely an issue even for novices. More adventurous river-runners find their rapid transit in challenging whitewater courses closer to the mountains.

3 Skiing & Snowboarding

Seattleites wait anxiously for the first large snowfall that carpets ski runs in the Cascades. Crystal Mountain, Alpental, Snoqualmie Pass, and Stevens Pass attract faithful downhill and crosscountry skiers, and boarders who have honed their skills on the area's famously challenging snow conditions.

Rock climbing walls, Stone Gardens

4 Burke-Gilman Trail

The legacy of two of Seattle's earliest railroad men, Judge Thomas Burke and Daniel Gilman, this disused railroad track is a paved trail *(see p84)* that stretches for about 22 miles (35 km) from the western edge of Fremont to the north end of Lake Washington. Cyclists and pedestrians can enjoy the scenic beauty of key sights such as GasWorks Park *(see p46)* and Magnuson Park at Sand Point.

5 Colman Pool

An alternative to cold, inhospitable Puget Sound is a dip in Colman Pool. It uses heated and filtered saltwater drawn from Puget Sound, which it overlooks from its convenient beach location within Lincoln Park *(see p47)*. *Map P2 • 8603 Fauntleroy Way SW • Adult $3.75, child/senior $2.75*

6 Highland Ice Arena

There's only one open-all-year ice rink that serves Seattle. It entertains legions of loyal customers including graceful figure skaters, daredevil hockey skaters, and families with young children just starting to learn the ropes. *Map P2 • 18005 Aurora Ave N • (206) 546-2431 • Adult/teen (13–64) $6; child/senior (6–12, 65+) $5.50*

If you bike the Burke-Gilman Trail, pay attention to the posted speed limits and keep right at all times.

7 Snowshoe Treks

A new trend in wintertime sports is snowshoeing, an ancient method of walking on or through the white stuff. The National Park Service and local outfitters offer a series of guided walks. Beginners should start with an experienced professional guide to lead the outing.

8 Scuba Diving

For an adventurous sport opt for scuba diving in Puget Sound to discover undersea creatures such as wolf eels, octopus, sea stars, and urchins with amazing ranges of size and color. Divers embark solo or as part of chartered excursions to take advantage of the coastline that's never victim to heavy damage or dangerous currents from Pacific Ocean storms.

9 Windsurfing

For one of the country's premier windsurfing meccas, you'll have to go to Hood River, Oregon, in the Columbia River Gorge. If extreme sports are not your style, Seattle has two prime locations for all who want to let the wind sweep them away — along the west shores of Lake Washington, between Magnuson Beach and Seward Park; and at Golden Gardens Park where Shilshole Bay meets Puget Sound.

10 Cycling Tolt-MacDonald Park & Campground

Many of Seattle's in-city parks have decent single tracks for casual-mountain biking. But for intermediate-level cyclists looking for small challenges in a great riverside setting, head east across Lake Washington for Carnation, in the Snoqualmie River valley, east of Redmond. *Map Q2 • 31020 NE 4th St*

Top 10 Places to Rent Gear

1 REI
This store helped define Seattle as an outdoor recreation mecca. *Map K2 • 222 Yale Ave N • (206) 223-1944*

2 Marmot Mountain Works
Stocks supplies for camping, skiing, and rock climbing. *Map L3 • 827 Bellevue Way NE, Bellevue • (425) 453-1515*

3 Feathered Friends
Has a great selection of climbing gear. *Map K2 • 119 Yale Ave N • (206) 292-2210*

4 Agua Verde Café & Paddle Club
Rent a kayak or dine on great Mexican food. *Map E2 • 1303 NE Boat St • (206) 545-8570*

5 Moss Bay Rowing & Kayaking Center
Offers a variety of kayaks and rowboats. *Map K1 • 1001 Fairview Ave N • (206) 682-2031*

6 Gregg's Greenlake Cycles
Hire ride bikes or inline skates here. *Map E1 • 7007 Woodlawn Ave NE • (206) 523-1822*

7 Alki Crab & Fish
Boat and kayak rentals and reasonable seafood on offer. *Map B5 • 1660 Harbor Ave SW • (206) 938-0975*

8 Windworks Sailing Center
Rent bareboats, or take sailing lessons. *Map A1 • 7001 Seaview Ave NW • (206) 784-9386*

9 Northwest Outdoor Center
Rent kayaks or paddle along the Canal. *Map D3 • 2100 Westlake Ave N • (206) 281-9694*

10 Center for Wooden Boats
(see p37)

Free maps of cycling routes are available at the city's Bicycle and Pedestrian Program: 600 4th Avenue, (206) 684-7583.

Left **GasWorks Park** Right **Woodland Park Rose Garden**

TOP 10 Urban Retreats

1 Greenlake

The well-worn paths in this lake's *(see p42)* sylvan setting take visitors around a placid lake in a quiet neighborhood north of downtown. Mirror-smooth or gently rippling with the wind, Greenlake's mesmerizing surface lets minds wander freely. It's packed on weekends, especially in summer months when sunbathers flock to the grassy areas for day-long solar treatments. *Map D1*

2 Volunteer Park

Between 1904 and 1909, the Olmsted Brothers turned these 45 acres of hilltop into a bucolic grass meadow with a fantastic view. The park now houses the Seattle Asian Art Museum *(see p36)*, the Volunteer Park Conservatory, and an observation tower *(see p72)*. It's also a notorious gay pick-up scene at night. *Map E3 • 1247 15th Ave E*

Volunteer Park Conservatory

3 GasWorks Park

Set up in 1906 as a gasification plant to light the streets of Seattle, this became the first industrial site in the world to be recreated into a public park. The park has been scrubbed several times over the years, much of the oversized, industrial machinery either remains on exhibit, or sits rusted and threatening like industrial mastodons behind high security fences. It has a high, grassy kite hill – topped with a sculptor's sundial. *Map D3 • 2101 N Northlake Way • (206) 684-4075*

4 Woodland Park Rose Garden

New visitors to the Woodland Park Zoo *(see pp24–25)* often bump into this gated area near one of the Zoo entrances. Others, nearly a quarter million annually, make sure to wake up and smell the roses. About 5,000 individual plants and 280 varieties of rose turn this 2.5-acre corner of north Seattle into a technicolor dream. *Map D1*

5 Schmitz Preserve Park

The scant remains of the temperate rainforest old growth trees give a clue of what Seattle must have resembled before European settlement. Schmitz is essentially a deep, wide, heavily wooded ravine surrounded by residential streets, but street noises disappear among the magnificent trees and native plantlife. *Map A5 • (206) 684-4075*

For safety reasons, Seattle parks close by 10pm or 11pm, and it's best not to visit them after dark.

6 Lake Washington Arboretum Japanese Garden

Stroll the Lake Washington Arboretum's 230 acres of carefully cultivated landscapes and rare tree species. The gardens, a living page of Japanese history, were built in 1960 according to plans by Japanese designer Juki Iida. These include a traditional sculpture, a stream, exotic flora, ponds, and a teahouse. *Map F4 • 1502 Lake Washington Blvd E • Adm*

7 Seattle Chinese Garden

Discover one of the largest Chinese gardens outside of China at the South Seattle Community College campus. Built by artisans from Seattle's sister city, Chongqing, the garden spans two separate cultures. Using horticulture, rocks, and water, the Sichuan-style garden integrates China's history, art and architecture, philosophy, and literature into a wondrous microcosm of the universe. *Map P3 • 6000 16th Ave SW • (206) 282-8040*

8 Center for Urban Horticulture

The University of Washington established the CUH in 1980 in order to exert more control and achieve sounder management of the Arboretum. It includes a library, a herb garden, pleasant strolling meadows, and weekly master gardener meetings. *Map F2 • 3501 NE 41st St*

Golden Gardens

9 Golden Gardens

In Ballard's far northwestern edge along Puget Sound, the wide sandy beaches of Golden Gardens *(see p90)* take on the characteristics of a cherished vacation spot. The Olympic Mountains stand to the west, a marina lies adjacent, and Lake Washington Ship Canal is nearby so pleasure crafts are always in view. There are two wetlands, a wooded area, a stream, and a loop trail. *Map P2*

10 Lincoln Park

On the road to West Seattle's Fauntleroy Ferry Terminal *(see p97)*, this is a versatile recreational find for those looking for hilly trails, picnics by the water, or even a dip in Colman Pool *(see p44)*. *Map P2*

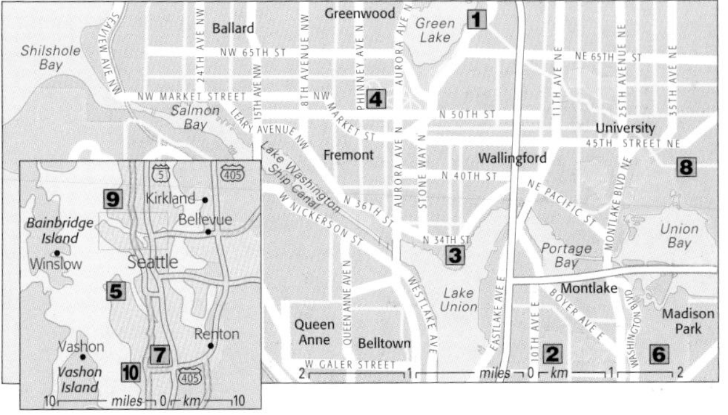

The Showbox

Top 10 Nightlife

1 The Showbox

This elegant 1900s Art Deco room with state-of-the-art audio and computer-controlled lighting has been used as a concert hall, a comedy club, and even a rental space for a Talmud Torah Hebrew Academy Bingo series. Artists as dissimilar as Al Jolson, the Mills Brothers, Gypsy Rose Lee, and the Ramones have performed here. Now, the 1,000-seat venue books successful touring rock and hip-hop acts. *Map J4 • 1426 1st Ave • (206) 628-0221*

2 Crocodile Café

This Belltown café opened in the early 1990s, just after major Seattle bands such as Nirvana, Soundgarden, and Mudhoney changed the face of rock music. It's still a destination for new talented bands, local or touring, appealing to audiences who favor college rock radio and singer-songwriters. Features inexpensive fare, and the owner's husband happens to be Peter Buck of R.E.M. *Map J3 • 2200 2nd Ave • (206) 441-5611 • $*

Crocodile Café

3 Chop Suey

This club dominates the smoke-filled, hard rock scene on Capitol Hill, but does so with style and flair. Glowing red lights and lanterns shed a bit of light, while images of Bruce Lee add to the kitschy theme. Most of the acts are local or regional rock outfits, although hip-hop rules on Sunday nights. *Map E4 • 1325 E Madison • (206) 324-8000*

4 Tractor Tavern

A bastion of great music, this place thrives as an alternative to clubs elsewhere in Seattle that are known for mining hard rock acts. The Tractor primarily books bands with repertoire in the vein of country western, rockabilly, bluegrass, or musicians who seamlessly fuse all those styles into something quite original. *Map B2 • 5213 Ballard Ave NW • (206) 789-3599*

5 Consolidated Works

The only multidisciplinary contemporary arts center in the Pacific Northwest is housed in a cavernous space large enough for jumbo jet assembly. ConWorks brings artists and patrons together with the philosophy that all creative art forms speak one language. The facility includes three artist-in-residence studios, a 150-seat theater, the 50-seat movie hall, a 6,000-ft (1,829-m) visual art space, and a café. *Map K2 • 500 Boren Ave N • (206) 381-3218*

Using the word "grunge" to describe Seattle's music will mark you as an unhip outsider or a journalist looking for verbal shortcuts.

6 Gallery 1412

If Gallery 1412's room is as small as ConWorks is gargantuan, the artistic vision is equally as imposing. The award-winning curators book acts dedicated to experimental music in a no-frills setting. Patrons listen and learn about contemporary composition, electroacoustic and electronic music, free improvization, and out jazz. *Map E5 • 1412 18th Ave • (206) 322-1533*

7 The Triple Door

In the space of a former 1920s-era vaudeville theater upscale audiences soak up the best of jazz, rock, cabaret, and blues while enjoying French wine and cuisine. *Map J4 • 216 Union St • (206) 838-4333*

8 El Corazón

Formerly known as Graceland, El Corazón proudly flaunts its roots as a crusty, smoky rock club. It's a mecca for those seeking strong drinks and a favorite venue for many of the area's hard-working rock bands. *Map L2 • 109 Eastlake Ave E • (206) 381-3094*

9 Sunset Tavern

This tavern is primarily an outlet for start-up bands of the ear-shattering punk rock persuasion. The room's red decor and lighting seems to take inspiration from a Victorian bordello. Lots of bands have their first gigs here. *Map B1 • 5433 Ballard Ave NW • (206) 784-4880*

10 Neumo's

The resurrected Moe's is now Neumo's, Capitol Hill's most hip and happening music venue. The club is back to basics with a strong show of rock bands and DJ dance nights. *Map M3 • 925 E Pike St • (206) 709-9467*

Top 10 Local Microbrews

1 Redhook

Seattle's earliest microbrewers began in May 1981. *Map P2 • 14300 NE 145th St*

2 Hale's Brewery

Savor delicious brews and pub grub. *Map C2 • 4301 Leary Way NW • (206) 706-1544*

3 Maritime Pacific

Order a pint of Nightwatch at this tavern. *Map C2 • 1514 NW Leary Way • (206) 782-6181*

4 Elliott Bay Brewing Company

West Seattle's bastion of microbrew and pub fare. *Map A6 • (206) 932-8695*

5 McMenamin's

This chain of pubs is known as Dad Watson's in Fremont. *Map D2 • 3601 Fremont Ave N • (206) 632-6505*

6 Elysian

The Hill's best pub makes legendary India pale ale and extra-special bitter. *Map M3 • 1221 E Pike St • (206) 860-1920*

7 Pyramid Alehouse, Brewery & Restaurant

Serves excellent beers and great faux-Egyptian label design too. *Map D6 • 1201 1st Ave S • (206) 682-3377*

8 Big Time Brewery & Alehouse

Draws young and old to sample handcrafted ales. *Map E2 • 4133 University Way NE • (206) 545-4509*

9 Pike Brewing Company

Best for microbrew, pub food, or brewing supplies. *Map J4 • 1415 1st Ave • (206) 622-6044*

10 Mac & Jack's

Try the African Amber for thirst-quenching nirvana. *Map P2 • 17825 NE 65th St, Redmond • (425) 558-9697*

The drinking age for all alcoholic beverages in Washington is 21, so have your ID handy when seeking entrance to taverns or bars.

Left **Metropolitan Grill** Right **Dahlia Lounge**

TOP 10 Restaurants

1 The Herbfarm

Dining at this Eastside restaurant requires time, money, and an appreciation of the culinary arts. Chef Jerry Traunfeld's kitchen often uses ingredients from the restaurant's gardens and farm. Creative menus include a nine-course dinner of Northwest foods, served with five or six matched wines (non alcoholic options are also available). Reserve well in advance. *Map P2 • 14590 NE 145th St, Woodinville • (206) 784-2222/ (425) 485-5300 • $$$$$*

2 Ray's Boathouse & Café

This Ballard waterfront restaurant has two dining rooms. The café caters to happy-hour revelers, families, and informal diners, while the boathouse is reservation-only seating. Both menus includes the freshest Dungeness crab, oysters, and wild salmon from Alaska. *Map A1 • 6049 Seaview Ave NW • (206) 782-0094 • $$*

3 Ponti Seafood Grill

Ponti creates sumptuous Pacific Rim dinners and hearty weekend brunches inside a Mediterranean-style villa. The chef fuses Asian herbs and spices with ahi tuna, scallops, and crab providing a harmonious meeting place for green curries and *les fruits de la mer*. *Map C2 • 3014 3rd Ave N • (206) 284-3000 • $$*

Dungeness crab

4 Metropolitan Grill

One of Seattle's most loved and traditional steak houses draws in a faithful cadre of politicians and corporate attorneys every day. Portions are typically huge – salads, appetizers, baked potatoes, everything – so bring lots of friends for sharing. *Map K5 • 820 2nd Ave • (206) 624-3287 • $$$*

5 Canlis

Treat your eyes and palate to dinner at Canlis. Specialties include Alaska halibut, Dungeness crab, Wasyugyu (Kobe) tenderloin, and a comprehensive and expensive wine selection. For a memorable occasion at Canlis reserve the private cache room for two, and order in advance to ensure a serving of the luscious chocolate lava cake. *Map D3 • 2576 Aurora Ave N • (206) 283-3313 • $$$*

6 Kaspar's

Both *Bon Appetit* and *Gourmet* magazines have praised the Swiss-born kitchen wizard, Kaspar Donier, who combines exotic flavors with local fish and seafood such as Penn Cove mussels, Alaskan king salmon, and crab dishes. For those undecided about dessert, there's a crowd-pleasing sampler for two or four people. The dining room is formal. *Map G2 • 19 W Harrison St • (206) 298-0123 • $$$*

For a guide to restaurant price ranges **See p68**

Le Gourmand façade

7 Wild Ginger
Wild Ginger's gourmet-meets-Asian cuisine offers such delicacies as satay and sauces, mango pork lamb satay, and soups. Its location across the street from Benaroya Hall *(see p38)* is spacious, so waits are not usually a problem unless you happen to arrive on a show night. *Map K4 • 1401 3rd Ave • (206) 623-4450 • $$*

8 Le Gourmand
Owner-chef Bruce Naftaly offers professional service and classic French cuisine featuring unusual, delicious dishes such as rabbit liver paté and shrimp mousseline. The desserts are tantalizing. *Map C1 • 425 NW Market St • (206) 784-3463 • $$$*

9 Rover's
Rover's caters to the city's most well-heeled and culinarily well-versed clientele. Owner-chef Thierry Rautureau and his staff create *prix fixe* five- and eight-course dinners. Rautureau's delicacies include fresh game, seafood, and classic sauces. *Map F4 • 2808 E Madison St • (206) 325-7442 • $$$$$*

10 Dahlia Lounge
Owner-chef Tom Douglas was one of the area's first fusion chefs, blending flavors into cohesive and tasty concoctions. Traditional dinner items such as crab cakes are favorites. Next door is the sweet-tooth's haven, Dahlia Bakery. *Map J3 • 2001 4th Ave • (206) 682-4142 • $$*

Top 10 Sushi Restaurants

1 Musashi's
This miniscule joint buzzes with customers as servings are generous and the price is astonishingly low. *Map D2 • 1400 N 45th St • (206) 633-0212*

2 Ototo
Caters to the sushi crowd with a stellar sake selection and slick service in an artistically designed shop. *Map C3 • 7 Boston St • (206) 691-3838*

3 Kozue
This place has its own loyal following. *Map D2 • 1608 N 45th St • (206) 547-2008*

4 Hana
Step in for the tastiest and least costly raw fish. *Map M2 • 219 Broadway E • (206) 328-1187*

5 Maneki
Try to reserve a private tatami room if you have a large group. *Map L6 • 304 6th Ave S • (206) 622-2631*

6 Shiro's
Seattle baseball superstar Ichiro dines here. *Map H3 • 2401 2nd Ave • (206) 443-9844*

7 Wasabi Bistro
Their tempura rolls are lavish and unique. *Map J3 • 2311 2nd Ave • (206) 441-6044*

8 Chiso
Serves imaginatively prepared sushi and sashimi. *Map D2 • 3520 Fremont Ave N • (206) 632-3430*

9 Azuma
Chef-owner prepares a small selection of fresh fish. *Map A6 • 4533 California Ave SW • (206) 937-1148*

10 I Love Sushi
This waterfront hideaway attracts crowds, as fish is always fresh. *Map K1 • 1001 Fairview Ave N • (206) 625-9604*

Please call in advance to check timings and closed days.

Left **Westlake Center exterior** Right **Westlake Center interior**

TOP 10 Stores & Shopping Centers

1 Pacific Place

Part of a $500 million development plan, this is the crown jewel of Seattle's retail shopping centers. Stores include Tiffany & Co., Coach, Ann Taylor, Helly Hansen, Cartier, Pottery Barn, L'Occitane, Aveda, and Williams-Sonoma. The top level has an 11-screen AMC Theatre complex and several fine gourmet restaurants. There is also a skybridge connection to Nordstrom's flagship store. *Map K4 • 600 Pine St • (206) 405-2655*

2 5th Avenue Boutiques

A collection of boutiques between Union and Spring Streets caters to customers for whom price is no object. Fox's Gem Shop, Brooks Brothers, and St. John Boutique are the best stops for fine gems and jewelry and high fashion galore. *Map K4*

Pacific Place shopping center

3 University Village

Renovated and repositioned as a stellar shopping destination this open-air mall just east of the UW has lovely landscaped walkways, fountains, restaurants, and stores that no longer attract just the resident graduate student population. Key stores include Abercrombie & Fitch, Barnes & Noble Booksellers, Restoration Hardware, and Banana Republic. *Map F2 • 4500 25th Ave NE • (206) 523-0622*

4 Westlake Center

The center has a four-tiered glass-enclosed atrium stacked with small regionally based shops, several chain stores, and a large food court. Made in Washington, April Cornell, Fossil, The Children's Place, Mont Blanc, and Talbots are well worth visiting. Outside, Westlake Plaza attracts workers on break and also features seasonal concerts and public events. *Map K4 • 400 Pine St • (206) 467-1600*

5 Nordstrom

John W. Nordstrom's *(see p31)* shoe store, opened with his Alaska Gold Rush earnings in 1901, is now synonymous with impeccable service and quality merchandise. Hunting for fine apparel, elegant shoes, exquisite handbags, or other fashion accessories can be exhausting, so step into the in-store spa and salon for an unusual experience. *Map K4 • 500 Pine St • (206) 628-2111*

Rainier Tower

6 Macy's

For less extravagant spenders, there's what used to be the locally owned Bon Marche. The new name reflects investment and ownership by the famous Chicago department store chain, but locals still refer to this large store simply as the Bon. Find everything from linen to lingerie, and loveseats to luggage, all at reasonable prices. *Map J4 • 300 Pine St • (206) 506-6000*

7 North of the Market to Belltown

A stroll along First and Second Avenues in the Belltown area leads to this ultrahip shopping destination, but you may witness remnants of some institutions along the way. Bushell's Auction, which has been in business since 1906, always has something of value for the right buyer. *Map J4 • 2006 2nd Ave*

8 Wallingford Center

For a real taste of Seattle's charming Wallingford neighborhood, discover a variety of local commerce along 45th Street, such as restaurants and shops, as well as the Wallingford Center, a converted turn-of-the-19th-century elementary school. Quite a few of these shops are for or about children, including L'il Klippers (haircuts), and The Tin Horse (children's toy store). *Map D2 • 1815 N 45th St • (206) 517-7773*

9 Rainier Square

A cavernous mini-city of upscale shops selling everything from imported chocolate to Louis Vuitton designer goods is in the base of Rainier Tower *(see p33)*. Find entrances on any of the four sides of the complex, which occupies an entire city block. Be sure to visit the Jeffrey Moose Gallery for the latest in painting and sculpture. The underground concourse links up with the Washington State Convention Center *(see p63)*. *Map K4 • 1310 4th Ave • (206) 373-7119*

10 Darbury Stenderu

One of Seattle's most original artist-designers, Stenderu's shop is a celebration of unusual color treatments and texture. Her hand-dyed silk, velvet, and light knits employ signature touches with woodcut prints and original paintings. Browse her famous collection of long gowns, or purchase more practical quilts and pillows. There's also a fine selection of scarves, hats, and bags. All items are one of a kind. *Map J4 • 2121 1st Ave • (206) 448-2625*

Left **Floating bridges** Right **Skyline of Bellevue**

TOP 10 The Eastside

1 Floating Bridges

Lake Washington's famous floating bridges, Interstate 90 and State Route 520, connect Seattle with Bellevue and the Eastside. Both highways resemble ordinary bridges except for the middle portions, which rest on the water's surface above air-filled pontoons that support tons of traffic and concrete. Occasional windstorms push waves of water onto the road, creating back-ups for commuters. *Map P2*

2 Kirkland

Once a small rural town across Lake Washington, Kirkland has grown into a sprawling suburb with resident Microsoft executives and managers giving it a reputation for expensive real estate. It's also known for a charming waterfront that offers great shopping and dining and fantastic beaches that provide views of Seattle and the Olympic Mountains. *Map P2*

3 Old Bellevue

Bellevue sometimes gets a bad rap from more city-slicked Seattleites. It's a classic suburb, as well as one of the state's largest cities. But there is an area that speaks of its former life as a small town. Head to Old Bellevue and its restored Main Street for the antidote to freeway interchanges and big box stores, especially if you like buying antiques. *Map P2*

4 Eastside Wineries

Tip your glass of red wine during a visit to Chateau Ste. Michelle, Washington state's oldest winery. Their 87-acre wooded estate in Woodinville, 15-miles (24-km) north of Seattle, hosts tours and well attended summer concerts. It's one of several outfits taking advantage of a climate that favors excellent grape varieties. Other producers of good quality wine include Columbia Crest, DeLille Cellars, and family owned and operated Facelli Winery. *Chateau Ste. Michelle: Map P2 • 14111 NE 145th St, Woodinville*

5 The Gates Estate

So many people wonder how and where one of the world's richest men lives. Microsoft's founder, Bill Gates, built his estate on Lake Washington's eastern shore installing the latest technological advancements in modern living – high-end security systems, customized touch and voice controls, and luxurious

A wine cellar

Marymoor Park

entertainment facilities. The estate is not open to the public, naturally, but it's visible from the water and touring boats occasionally cruise within sight from a considerable distance. *Map P2 • 1835 73rd Ave NE, Medina*

6 Crossroads Shopping Center

This bustling shopping center is popular with Microsoft employees and vibrant ethnic groups, sometimes in traditional regalia. Free jazz, folk, and world music concerts on a professional stage and public art installations help make this a gathering place with personality. *Map P2 • 15600 NE 8th St • (425) 644-1111*

7 Mercer Slough Nature Park

This 300-acre park on the grounds of the largest remaining wetland on Lake Washington has a 5-mile (8-km) network of trails and esplanades. Bird-watchers flock to the Slough to view 100 species; other wildlife includes coyote, beaver, and muskrat. Activities comprise canoeing and kayaking, guided nature walks, and u-pick blueberries during the summer season. *Map P2 • 2102 Bellevue Way SE, Bellevue*

8 Marymoor Park

The county's most popular park, located in Redmond, maintains soccer and baseball fields, a velodrome, and an off-leash dog-training field. Dogs are free to roam and splash in water, a practice seriously discouraged or outlawed everywhere else. Park trails connect with the Sammamish River Trail, a bike route that leads to popular wineries in Woodinville. *Map P2 • 6046 W Lake Sammamish Pkwy NE, Redmond*

9 Luther Burbank Park

Mercer Island is a small affluent community off Interstate 90 near Lake Washington's eastern shore. The lovely waterfront park, on the northeastern tip of the island, offers boaters and visitors notable attractions such as tennis courts, a playground, and trails that lead to a swimming area and fishing dock. On summer Sunday afternoons, the park hosts free concerts in its amphitheater. *Map P2 • 2040 84th Ave SE, Mercer Island*

10 Dinner Train

An engaging way to travel up the lake to the Washington State wineries between Renton and Woodinville is on this vintage train that presents dinner and shows. The cuisine and scenery combine for a great but brief taste of the golden age of rail travel. The Spirit of Washington departs from Renton. *Spirit of Washington: Map P3 • 625 S 4th St (Renton) • (425) 227-7245*

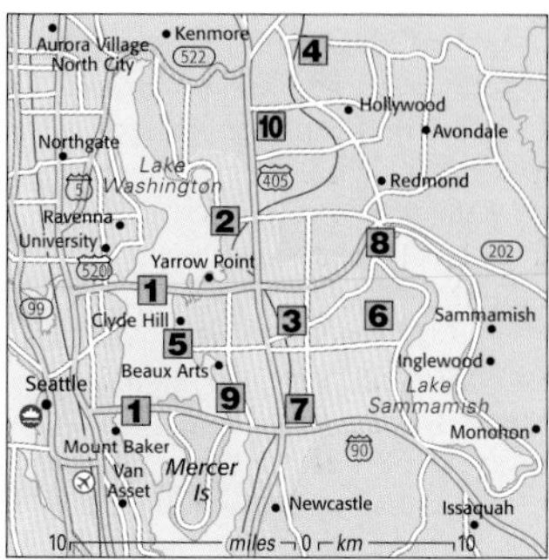

Left **San Juan Island** Center **Lighthouse, Pt. Townsend** Right **Ann Starrett Mansion, Pt. Townsend**

Top 10 Day Trips: Islands & Historic Towns

1 Bainbridge Island

The ferry ride to Winslow on Bainbridge Island should be mandatory for tourists who want an inspiring view of the Seattle skyline. A stroll from the terminal to Winslow's quaint waterfront shops and cafés has its own rewards. *Map N2 • 590 Winslow Way E • (206) 842-3700*

2 Vashon Island

Vashon's gentle, two-lane roads make it a favorite destination for both bicyclists and motorcyclists looking for a quick and unique getaway to the countryside. Board the Fauntleroy Ferry *(see p97)* in West Seattle to discover the island's huge estates, arts and craft galleries, berry and llama farms, and a subculture of 1960s-style progressives. *Map N3*

3 Whidbey Island

As the longest island in the western contiguous United States, Whidbey Island's ample waterfront real estate makes it vacation-home central. The island's five state parks, historic forts, and tiny seaside villages attract weekend crowds. It is also the perfect location for the area's largest US Navy air base. Their sign reads, "Pardon our noise, it's the sound of freedom". *Map P1*

4 San Juan Islands

In the far northwest of Washington state lies the San Juan archipelago, comprising 700 islands of which only 177 have names. Ferries sail from Anacortes to the four largest islands – Lopez, Shaw, San Juan, and Orcas. Lopez is great for cycling. Hilly Orcas offers breathtaking views from atop Mt. Constitution. At 2,409 ft (734 m), it provides the best viewpoint of the area's stunning geographical features. San Juan, with the largest town (Friday Harbor) is best for walk-on passengers. Be sure to check out the Whale Museum if you visit. Shaw Island does not offer visitor facilities. *Map N4*

5 Tacoma

Founded as a sawmill town in the 1860s, Tacoma is known for its historic buildings and strong architectural symbols, which includes the 1893 Italianate tower of Old City Hall. The impressive Chihuly Bridge of Glass links the Museum of Glass to downtown Tacoma and the imaginative Washington State History Museum. Explore the small but impressive Tacoma Art Museum, and Point Defiance Zoo and Aquarium, highlighting a Pacific Rim theme. *Map P3*

Tacoma Museum of Glass

If you need a ferry and prefer not to miss the boat, avoid rush hours and arrive at least 45 minutes before ferry departure.

6 Leavenworth

In an effort to revive the dying logging town, civic leaders came up with the German theme in the 1970s. The town with its Bavarian-styled architecture now bustles with festivals, art shows, and summer theater productions. Another popular attraction is the Leavenworth Nutcracker Museum. *Map Q5*

Horse-drawn beer wagon, Leavenworth

7 Olympia

Washington's state capital has a rich past, historic buildings, and a thriving youth culture. Highlights include the State Capitol Campus, with grounds designed by the Olmsted Brothers in 1928, Evergreen State University, a farmers' market, and the surrounding mostly rural Thurston County. *Map P5 • 103 14th Ave SW*

8 Roslyn

The model for Cicely, Alaska, in the television show, *Northern Exposure*, Roslyn has its own history unrelated to the quirky profiles offered in Hollywood's depiction. In this mining boomtown, late-19th century coal companies imported workers of various nationalities, as is evident from the tombs in the cemetery, grouped as they are in 26 'segregated' areas. Roslyn is on the National Historic Register. *Map Q6*

9 Port Townsend

This idyllic seaport, on the northeast tip of the Olympic Peninsula, attracts artists and musicians. Known for its Victorian architecture, key sights include Jefferson County Historical Society, Ann Starrett Mansion, Fire Bell Tower, and Fort Worden State Park. The small town has a bustling waterfront with shops, cafés, restaurants, and a ferry terminal. *Map N1*

10 Victoria, BC

Catch a ferry or seaplane to British Columbia's provincial capital, Victoria. Established as a Hudson's Bay Company fur-trading post in 1843, it has become a favorite destination for Anglophiles who queue up at the grand Fairmont Empress Hotel for traditional tea and cakes. Other attractions include the Inner Harbour, the Royal British Columbia Museum, and Butchart Gardens – an amazing collection of flora planted in a sprawling former quarry. *Map N4*

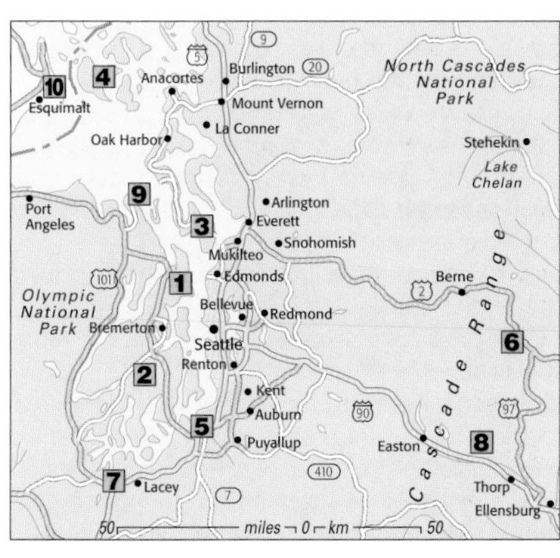

For more information on ferry departures call (206) 464-6400 or log onto www.wsdot.wa.gov/ferries

Hikers at Paradise, Mount Rainier

Top 10 Day Trips: Mountain Getaways

1 Mount Rainier

This silent, snowcapped sentinel, the centerpiece of Mount Rainier National Park, is an awe-inspiring active volcano rising 14,410-ft (4,392-m) above sea level. Since the cataclysmic explosion of Mount St. Helens in 1980, the Grand Dame of the Cascades commands new respect for its potentially devastating force. *Map P6*

View of Mount Rainier

2 Mount Si

Seattle's closest Cascade Mountain, the rocky outcropping of Mount Si is just past Issaquah. The hike is steep but not too difficult, and the views of the Snoqualmie Valley watershed and I-90 are rewarding. *Map Q5*

3 Issaquah Alps

This series of foothills west of the Cascades are remnants of mountains that predate the higher and more visited peaks to the east. Cougar, Squak, Tiger, and Rattlesnake Mountains are four main park areas that attract individuals and families seeking woodland walks without steep drops or high altitude. *Map P3*

4 Snoqualmie Falls

Local Native American tribes regarded Snoqualmie Falls as a sacred place. The 276-ft (84-m) waterfall, beautifully divided in two sections by a convenient rock outcropping, marks the end of the Cascade Plateau, where the Snoqualmie River begins its final descent to the sea. An observation deck and a steep path to the river allow for close-up breathtaking views. *Map Q3*

5 Twin Falls

Hikers wanting a short spell of deep woods and water head to Olallie State Park, where a 3-mile (5-km) trail to Twin Falls awaits. The park's amazing plant life includes giant ferns and salmonberry, and some of the Cascades' few old-growth trees. One Douglas fir has a circumference of 14 ft (4 m). *Map Q5*

6 Denny Creek

Hiking near Snoqualmie Pass along I-90 is a mecca for families with kids. The creek pours over a series of rocks and creates pools for perfect old-fashioned swimming hole fun. *Map Q5*

7 Tonga Ridge

The 6.5-mile (10-km) trail in the Alpine Lakes Wilderness offers a pleasant walk through forests and wild berry picking when the season's right. Meadows bloom in a kaleidoscope of colors in late spring, and mountain scenery abounds. *Map Q5*

Carry proper supplies for hiking in the mountains. **See p45**

Snoqualmie Falls

8 Staircase Rapids
The ferry crossing and subsequent scenic drive along the Hood Canal enhance the journey to these rapids. The popular route inches near the fast-flowing Skokomish River as it pours down the eastern slopes of the Olympic Range on its way to Lake Cushman. Look out for kingfishers, harlequin ducks, and giant salamanders on the 2-mile (3-km) loop. *Map N5*

9 Hurricane Ridge
Drive to this 5,230-ft (1,594-m) mountain top at one of Olympic National Park's most visited sites. The routes are paved, and bring visitors to one of the best 360-degree alpine overlooks. In winter, when the snowpack is immensely deep, the roads remain open for skiers and snowshoers. *Map N5*

10 Big Four Ice Caves
Global warming has taken a toll on ice caves, but the attraction at the base of 6,153-ft (1,875-m) Big Four Mountain in the North Cascades is still vital. Hike the 1-mile (1.6-km) trail off the Mountain Loop Highway to the Ice Caves, the unusual result of alpine avalanches and climate conditions impacting the ice field at the mountain's base. *Map P5*

Top 10 Features of Mount Rainier

1 Paradise
Leads to wildflower-filled meadows, and trails starting at 5,400-ft (1,646-m) to moraines and majestic views of the Nisqually Glacier.

2 Sunrise
Recommended as starting point for solitary hikes.

3 Summit Climb
A round-trip to the crater and back requires training, professional gear, and a few days. Hire a guide or go with a group if you're not a seasoned climber.

4 Family Day Hikes
Dozens of trails for family day trips and picnics are available; try one out near the Carbon River entrance.

5 Wonderland Trail
This 93-mile (149-km) trail through several mini-ecosystems around the mountain is ideal for serious backpackers with weeks to spare.

6 Cloud Lid
Rainier's cloud cover often resembles a flying saucer hovering above the peak.

7 Glacial Melting
Climate changes have decreased the area of Rainier's permanent snow cap and facilitated glacial retreats.

8 Jökulhlaups & Lahars
Glacial floods and debris flows can move at speeds up to 60 mph (95.5 km/h).

9 Sleeping Giant
Experts agree that it's a question of when, and not if, Mount Rainier's active volcano will blow again.

10 Pollution's Effects
Smog from automobile traffic now obscures the mountain more and more.

Contact nearby ranger stations for trail passes and information.

PIONEER BUILDING
PIONEER SQUARE MALL
COLLECTIBLES.ETC.
ANTIQUES

AROUND TOWN

Left **Pike Place Market** Center **Totem poles, Pioneer Square** Right **Elliott Bay Book Company**

Downtown

WHAT STRIKES MANY VISITORS to downtown Seattle is how easy it is to see the sights, since key attractions lie within walking distance of one another. Bookended by Belltown to the north and Pioneer Square to the south, downtown can be seen on foot or by city bus at no cost – since all of it lies in the Ride Free Zone. Alternatively, for a small fare, the waterfront streetcar stops at several key points between the Market and the International District. In addition to being a business district full of skyscrapers, downtown offers a wide range of options – such as gourmet restaurants, attractive shopping centers, and a perfect place to begin exploring the city.

Left **Rachel, the Market pig** Right **Pike Place Market stalls**

Top 10 Sights

1. Pike Place Market
2. Seattle Art Museum
3. Harbor Steps
4. Washington State Convention Center/ Freeway Park
5. Bank of America Tower
6. Pioneer Square
7. Koolhaas Library
8. Monorail
9. Belltown
10. Metro Bus Tunnel/ Ride Free Zone

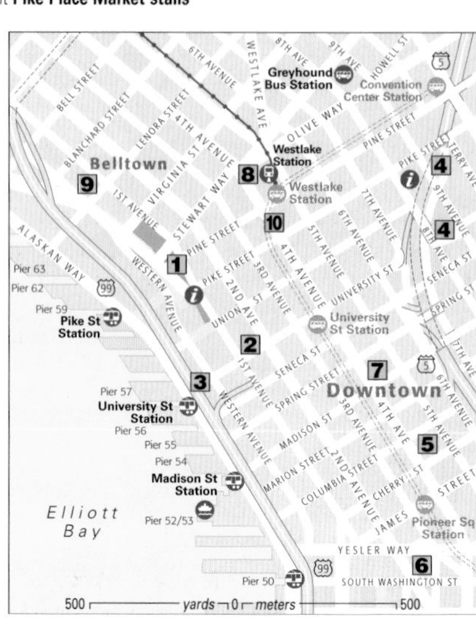

Previous pages **Totem pole at Pioneer Square**

Fish-flinging fishmongers

1 Pike Place Market

Anyone descending on Pike Place Market to stroll by innumerable stalls of seafood, fresh produce, crafts, and flower bouquets can feel the rapid pulse of a scene that's all about hard work and hustle. The Market is famous for its salmon-throwing fishmongers and street musicians who entertain tourists daily. *See pp8–9.*

2 Seattle Art Museum

Designed by Venturi Scott Brown and Associates, the imposing sandstone and limestone edifice houses an enviable permanent collection of about 23,000 pieces. The African collection inspires with traditional sculpture, masks, textiles, basketry, and decorative arts. The John Hauberg Collection, one of the most prized examples of Northwest Coastal Native American art, comprises nearly 200 artifacts from British Columbia, Alaska, Washington, and Oregon. The museum is undergoing extensive refurbishment until spring 2007. The construction of a new Olympic Sculpture Park in downtown Seattle is also underway. *See p36.*

3 Harbor Steps

If you happen to be near the Seattle Art Museum on First Avenue and need to get down to the waterfront, try the Harbor Steps. A street's abrupt end has been turned into a wide-open stairway landscaped with water sculpture and planters. The steps are spacious and an ideal urban meeting place, located below a nouveau luxury apartment complex in the heart of an ever-changing downtown Seattle. Countless restaurant and nightlife options abound in the vicinity. *Map J5*

4 Washington State Convention Center/ Freeway Park

Straddling Interstate 5 in a miraculous feat of engineering, the Washington State Convention Center is located within easy walking distance of the city's best shops, hotels, and restaurants. Marvel at the center's 90-ft (27-m) wide glass canopy bridge that frames views to Elliott Bay and to the historic Pike-Pine neighborhood. Adjoining is Freeway Park, where blossoms delight visitors in spring and waterfalls mask the sounds of traffic flowing on all sides. *Washington State Convention Center: Map K4; 800 Convention Place; (206) 694-5000; www.wsctc.com • Freeway Park: Map K4*

Washington State Convention Center

Many seafood vendors at Pike Place Market package fish for long-distance travel.

The tall, black Columbia Tower

5 Columbia Tower

The sleek, three-tiered black skyscraper that dominates Seattle's skyline might have been even taller, but for an order to reduce the ultimate height from the Federal Aviation Administration. To break a record for most floors in any one building, the builder kept the original 76 stories but reduced the ceiling heights to compensate. The 1985 building has an observation deck on the 73rd floor that offers panoramic views of Elliott Bay and Mount Rainier. *See p32.*

6 Pioneer Square

Find art galleries, intricate Victorian architecture, bookstores, and cafés in a constantly changing National Historic District. Pioneer Square's 20-block neighborhood became Seattle's commercial center during the boom years of logging, fishing, railroads, and Klondike Gold Rush economies. An exclusive 90-minute underground tour *(see p14)* offers a lively look at the 19th-century storefronts that were periodically flooded by tides from Elliott Bay until street levels were raised. Key sights include the Smith Tower, Elliott Bay Book Co. and Café, and an art walk on the first Thursday night of each month. *Map K5*

7 Koolhaas Library

Completed in 2004, the new downtown library is a work of art. Nearly 8,000 patrons per day benefit from more than 1.45 million books and reference materials, Internet access, spacious areas for children, and over 400 public computers. The art collection alone is worth $1 million. *See p32.*

8 Monorail

In 2005, Monorail services were suspended due to a collision between trains. By mid 2007 you'll be able to hop aboard once again to experience the future of mass transit from the perspective of engineers who built the elevated rail as an attraction for the 1962 World's Fair. The Monorail travels speedily and nonstop for 1.2 miles (2 km) between Seattle Center and Westlake Center. *See pp11 & 32.*

Denny Regrade

Named after one of the city's founders, Arthur A. Denny, Denny Hill would have certainly become one of Seattle's most upscale neighborhoods, with magnificent city, mountain, and water views. However, in 1905, engineers began its outright removal by extracting the mud with water jets and conveyor belts, eventually dumping the debris into Elliott Bay. Today, the unnaturally flat, 50-square-block area includes most of what's now called Belltown, and is occupied largely by warehouses, labor union halls, motels, and car lots.

Head inside the Koolhaas Library for a visual treat as spectacular as the glass and steel exterior shell.

Monorail at Seattle Center Station

9 Belltown

Pedestrians are welcomed with an explosion of shops, clubs, cafés, luxury condos, and fine restaurants. This upscale neighborhood was named in the 1970s after a pioneer, William M. Bell. In those days, Belltown attracted sailors on shore leave, artists seeking inexpensive loft spaces, and ragtag urban dwellers. But it was the dot.com boom of the 1990s that changed everything by engendering a commercial revival for the neighborhood. Remnants of old Belltown include a few well-preserved façades. *Map J4*

10 Ride Free Zone

The downtown sightseeing area between Belltown and Pioneer Square falls within the city's Ride Free Zone where fares are gratis. Hop on a street level bus within the Zone and don't forget to check in with the driver. All stations in the Downtown Seattle Transit Tunnel *(see p33)* are within the Ride Free Zone but during tunnel closure buses along 3rd Avenue are free between 6–9am and 3–6pm, and the Ride Free Zone is extended to include the stops at 9th Avenue and Howell Street. *Map K3*

Downtown Shopping Spree

Mid-morning

Stop at **Westlake Center** *(see p52)* and grab an espresso and pastry at the stand in the plaza before window-shopping Westlake's indoor mall. Inside, **Made in Washington** offers a large and creative inventory of regionally produced merchandise. Walk across Pine Street to find **Nordstrom's** spacious flagship store *(see p52)*, stocked with top designer brands and the absolute best of everything. Splurge in **Pacific Place** mall *(see p52)*, where you can choose from upmarket stores including Tiffany & Co., Coach, Ann Taylor, Cartier, and Williams-Sonoma. Exit the mall on Pine, turn right, and then left on 5th Avenue to University Street for pricey boutiques and fine jewelry, such as **Fox's Gem Shop** (1341 5th Ave).

Descend into the cavernous indoor mall at **Rainier Square** *(see p53)*, underneath the white high-rise that rests on a narrow pedestal. The base of the building opens up for a city block's worth of shops, galleries, and restaurants. Look for fine art in the **Jeffrey Moose Gallery** and imported Swiss chocolate from **Neuhaus**. Walk downhill on University to 4th Avenue, where you can board a number of non-express buses for a free ride back to Pike Street, or stay on the bus a few more blocks to Virginia Street for a superb Italian lunch at **Assaggio** *(see p67)*. Ask the driver for help if you need it.

Be sure to leave the bus while still in the Ride Free Zone; if you stay on beyond the boundary, you'll have to pay upon exiting.

Left **Waterfront streetcar** Right **Austin A. Bell Building**

Top 10 Around Belltown

1 Lenora Street Bridge
This elegant footbridge leads from Western Avenue to the Elliott Bay piers, providing stellar views of West Seattle and the Olympic Mountains. *Map H4*

2 Whiskey Bar
This trendy yet comfortable bar in Belltown offers a large variety of whiskey. Good for pre-concert gatherings due to its proximity to the Moore Theatre. *Map J4 • 2000 2nd Ave*

3 Belltown Billiards
A mix of professional-quality billiard tables with sumptuous Italian fare, DJs, and live music creates a hopping late-night scene. *Map H4 • 90 Blanchard St*

4 Rendezvous
This bar houses the miniscule Jewel Box Theater, a 1926-era private movie screening room, while the remodeled bar draws hipsters and condo dwellers. *Map H3 • 2320 2nd Ave*

5 TopPot Doughnuts
Take a hiatus from healthful dining and grab a few doughnuts from this stylish cafe' that welcomes loungers sipping coffee and dipping tasty treats. *Map J3 • 2124 5th Ave*

6 Sub Pop World Headquarters
The local record label created by Jonathan Poneman and Bruce Pavitt in the mid-1980s signed bands such as Nirvana and Soundgarden that put Seattle on the rock music map worldwide. *Map H3 • 2013 4th Ave*

7 Waterfront Station
For a picturesque journey while heading to Pioneer Square or the International District, board the waterfront streetcar. There're stations near Belltown at the foot of Vine and Bell Streets, near Piers 66, 67, and 69.

8 Austin A. Bell Building
Elmer Fisher, Seattle's foremost commercial architect, designed this handsome building that reflects Richardsonian, Gothic, and Italianate styles. It houses pricey condos and a nightclub. *Map H3 • 2326 1st Ave*

9 Art Institute of Seattle
The institute offers programs in graphics, fashion, and culinary and media arts. *Map H4 • 2323 Elliott Ave • (206) 448-0900*

10 Millionaire's Club
This social service agency helps potential laborers find temporary work. *Map H3*

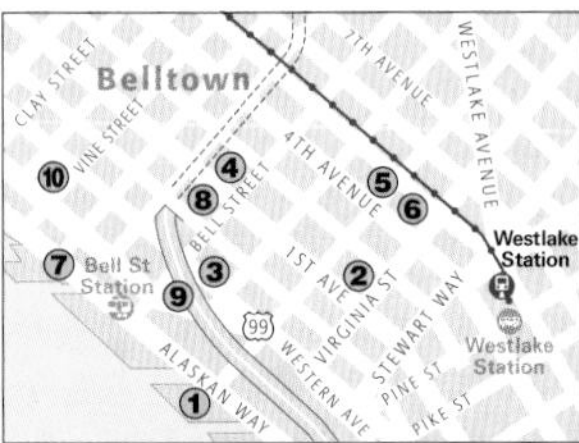

As a general rule, keep your distance from transients, panhandlers, and strangers with drunken pleas.

Price Categories

Price categories include a three-course meal for one, two glasses of wine and all unavoidable extra charges including tax		
	$	under $20
	$$	$20–$40
	$$$	$40–$55
	$$$$	$55–$80
	$$$$$	over $80

Left **Two Bells Tavern** Right **Crocodile Café**

TOP 10 Belltown Places to Eat

1 Mistral
Known for its formal atmosphere and haute cuisine, the Mistral has *prix-fixe* tasting menus featuring delicacies such as asparagus and English pea fricassee, or artisanal seared foie gras. *Map J3 • 113 Blanchard St • (206) 770-7799 • $$$$$*

2 Cyclops
Local customers return for their classic hummus plate, and both *Interview* and *Details* magazines have raved about the scene. Don't miss the roast chicken quesadilla. *Map H3 • 2421 1st Ave • (206) 441-1677 • $*

3 Assaggio Ristorante
Savor tasty authentic Italian cuisine such as fresh herbed veal parmigiana, ravioli cappesante, gnocchi gorgonzola, and osso buco. Many desserts are imported from Italy. *Map J3 • 2010 4th Ave • (206) 441-1399 • $$*

4 Dahlia Lounge
(see p51)

5 Queen City Grill
Treat yourself to a softly lit dining room, superb cocktails, great dishes such as grilled fish or lamb chops, and live jazz. *Map J4 • 2201 1st Ave • (206) 443-0975 • $$*

6 Two Bells Tavern
Great pub grub, especially burgers, and microbrews on tap. Occasional live music. *Map J3 • 2313 4th Ave • (206) 441-3050 • $*

7 Crocodile Café
The funky bar *(see p48)* that forms the epicenter of Seattle's rock scene features inexpensive fare typical of standard diners and pubs. It's also a great place to check out tattoos.

8 Belltown Pizza
A neighborhood bar? A pizzeria? Standard pizzas and gourmet varieties complement a small pasta selection, which may include dishes such as gorgonzola and walnut-stuffed ravioli in a garlic cream sauce. *Map H3 • 2422 1st Ave • (206) 441-2653 • $*

9 Macrina Bakery
A cherished bakery café famous for bread pudding with fresh cream and berries, soups, salads, and sandwiches. *Map H3 • 2408 1st Ave • (206) 448-4032 • $*

10 Brasa
Diners in the informal lounge may choose from steak frites, pizzas, fried oysters, and pasta. Take the time for lavish offerings such as lamb tagine or cumin-dusted sea scallops. *Map J3 • 2107 3rd Ave • (206) 728-4220 • $$$*

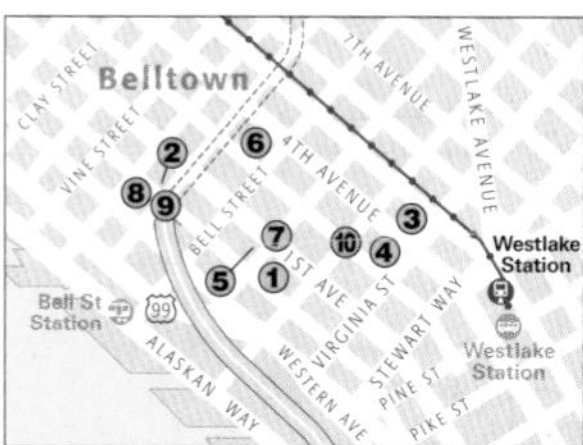

Unless otherwise noted, all restaurants accept major credit cards and can accommodate vegetarians.

Left **E.E. Robbins sign** Right **Seattle Cellars**

Top 10 Belltown Shops

1 Baby & Co.
The place for European styled slacks, skirts, dresses, and accessories for women. Look for designs by Martha Francis Garbed, Lilt in Paris, Comme des Garcons, and Marithe and Francois Girbaud. *Map J4 • 1936 1st Ave*

2 Paperhaus
Shop for contemporary presentation supplies and storage materials from award-winning manufacturers such as NAVA, Prat, and Rexite. Unique binders or photo albums are also available. *Map J4 • 2008 1st Ave*

3 Vain
An innovative one-stop shop for hip consumers who need to mainline trendiness. Discover a full service salon, beauty supply store, independent designer boutique, and an artist gallery. *Map J4 • 2018 1st Ave*

4 Patagonia
Its roots as purveyor of first-rate gear, rugged wear, and polar fleece comfort began with alpinist and founder Yvon Chouinard. *Map J4 • 2100 1st Ave*

5 E.E. Robbins Engagement Rings
It would be hard to miss the arty neon sign of a bejeweled ring glowing above this tempting shop in Belltown. The staff is informed and easy going. *Map J4 • 2200 1st Ave*

6 Karan Dannenberg Couture
Offers original and elegant wear for the sophisticated shopper, but expect the silk suits and lace-trimmed casual items to be expensive. *Map J4 • 2232 1st Ave*

7 Endless Knot
Stocking sizes small to 3X, this popular shop marries elegance with the unusual. Artful designs with a contemporary Asian feel. *Map H3 • 2300 1st Ave*

8 Riflessi
Fine handmade *objets d'art* and decorative tableware from Italian studios that pride themselves on preserving artistic integrity, traditional techniques, and using the best materials available. *Map H3 • 2302 1st Ave*

9 Seattle Cellars
The store stocks an enviable selection of reds, whites, and sparkling wine, and the layout makes searching by region easy. The staff is proficient in recommending wines no matter what your budget is. *Map H3 • 2505 2nd Ave • Wine tasting: Thu from 5–7pm*

10 Carol McClellan
Visitors can select the fabric and color for a custom leather dress or jacket. Joining the hip set may cost you up to $2,700 for a two-piece suit, while armbands are merely $45. *Map H3 • 103 Battery St*

Save space in your luggage by asking stores to ship your purchases to your home or office.

Left **Eddie Bauer** Right **Borders bookstore**

Top 10 Downtown Shops

1 Pendleton
Thomas Kay founded this popular retail outlet specializing in blankets, and clothes for men and women. *Map K4 • 1313 4th Ave*

2 Jeri Rice
Bargain shoppers may need to wait for the annual sale of women's clothes in January. Otherwise, bask in luxurious threads from designers such as Dusan, Sonia Rykiel, Yves St. Laurent, Clara Cottman, and Gaultier. *Map K4 • 421 University St • www.jeririce.com*

3 Mariners Team Store
Here's where to purchase official team jerseys and t-shirts, baseball caps, and other gift items emblazoned with the Seattle's winning professional league team logo. *Map J4 • 1800 4th Ave*

4 Coldwater Creek
This spacious home furnishing and clothing store welcomes shoppers with hardwood floors, a stream, and a waterfall. *Map K4 • 1511 5th Ave • www.coldwatercreek.com*

5 Betsey Johnson
Every fashionable young woman who's flirty and flouncy knows of the designer who helped create the image of the Warhol crowd's Edie Sedgewick. Examine the sale rack before you buy. *Map K4 • 1429 5th Ave • www.betseyjohnson.com*

6 Eddie Bauer
This store offers seasonal collections of all-occasion apparel, footwear, travel gear, and accessories for men and women. Founded in 1920 in Seattle, today more than 425 stores exist worldwide. *Map K4 • 1330 5th Ave • www.eddiebauer.com*

7 Nancy Meyer
Supplement your purchases of trendy outerwear with lingerie that's as sexy as it is elegant and tasteful. *Map K4 • 1318 5th Ave*

8 Isadora's
New, designer, vintage, and private label, Isadora's collection of imaginative clothing and estate jewelry has been a hit for more than 30 years. Lots of incredible and ultra *luxe* finds. *Map J4 • 1915 1st Ave*

9 Peter Miller
A specialty bookstore that makes you feel sleek and creative. Scout for anything on architecture, graphic design, landscaping, and art in general, or Corbu letter stencils, planners, business-card holders, and art-imbibed gift items. *Map J4 • 1930 1st Ave • www.petermiller.com*

10 Borders
The large book and music CD retailer has an unparalleled inventory of popular books, magazines, and compact discs. *Map K4 • 1501 4th Ave • www.bordersstores.com*

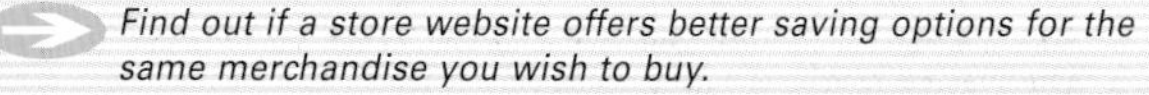

Find out if a store website offers better saving options for the same merchandise you wish to buy.

Left **A nightlife scene, Neighbors** Center **St. Mark's Episcopal Cathedral** Right **Seattle pastime**

Capitol Hill

DISCOVER ONE OF SEATTLE'S *most electrifying neighborhoods on the long ridge that stretches northeast of downtown. The large gay, lesbian, and transgendered resident population helped to create a vibrant culture reflected in street scenes that hover on the outside edge of mainstream society. But Capitol Hill is much more than a magnet for self expression, although you may see more dyed and spiked hair and imaginatively applied body piercings than elsewhere in Seattle. Abundant shops, clubs, restaurants, and cafés along Broadway, Pike and Pine Streets, and 15th Avenue East draw crowds from all over the city. Key attractions include two vintage movie theaters – the Harvard Exit and the Egyptian Theater – the Cornish College of the Arts, the Central Seattle Community College, and the Seattle Asian Art Museum in the sylvan setting of Volunteer Park. There are quiet streets nearby that boast some of the most lavish private residences in Seattle.*

Comet Tavern sign

TOP 10 Sights

1. Broadway
2. Pike/Pine Corridor
3. Cathedrals
4. Gay/Lesbian Scene
5. Hendrix Statue
6. Richard Hugo House
7. Volunteer Park Observation Tower
8. Lake View Cemetery
9. Neighborhood Homes
10. Eastlake

On most western Capitol Hill streets, downhill is west, uphill is east. Numbered streets run north–south.

Coffee shops on Broadway

1 Broadway

If you can buy it, you can find it on Broadway, the nerve center of Capitol Hill. From East Pike to East Roy Streets, storefronts beckon consumers on the hunt for food, vintage and new clothing, music CDs, and lots of coffee. On summer evenings especially, the sheer density of pedestrian traffic along Broadway matches that of midtown Manhattan. *See pp18–19.*

2 Pike/Pine Corridor

Bisecting Capitol Hill are two busy streets offering their own flavor and subculture. You can find many of the area's gay and lesbian hangouts on the blocks above and below Broadway, as well as a great selection of taverns and stores selling vintage housewares and furnishings. Although the city has tried to discourage their postings, you may also notice colorful flyers stapled onto telephone poles and virtually any surface, advertising band concerts in the vicinity. If nothing else, they draw attention to the pulse that keeps this community living and breathing on the edge. *Map E4*

3 Cathedrals

Capitol Hill has a number of landmark places of worship, including the grand St. Mark's Episcopal Cathedral, which belongs to the Diocese of Olympia. Organ enthusiasts come from afar to play St. Mark's 3,944-pipe Flentrop organ, installed in 1965. The Saint Nicholas Russian Orthodox Cathedral, one of the oldest parishes of the Russian Orthodox Church outside of Russia, was founded in 1930 by immigrants who fled the 1917 Russian Revolution. The structure's ornate turquoise *lukovitsa* (16th century "onion dome" style of cupolas) and spires rise high above the trees and neighboring homes. *St. Mark's Episcopal Cathedral: Map E4; 1245 10th Ave E • St. Nicholas Russian Orthodox Cathedral: Map E4; 1714 13th Ave*

4 Gay/Lesbian Scene

Alternative lifestyles are not only tolerated, but encouraged with flagrant same-sex smooching and handholding on the streets. Gay and lesbian clubs *(see p74)* proliferate on the Hill, as do shops selling what used to be called marital aids — sex toys in today's parlance.

Street youth living on or near Broadway's environs are largely harmless. Use your best judgment if they ask for spare change.

5 Hendrix Statue

Darryl Smith, an artist once based at the Fremont Fine Arts Foundry, created a lifesize bronze statue of Jimi Hendrix that now graces the Pine Street sidewalk. It shows the musician in his trademark rockstar pose, kneeling in bellbottoms with his Fender guitar pointed skyward. Before Paul Allen built his Experience Music Project *(see pp10 & 32)*, inspired by Hendrix and his music, this installation was Seattle's best known memorial dedicated to the city's famous guitarist. *Map M3*

6 Richard Hugo House

Writers and readers have enthusiastic support from this institution, named for Richard Hugo (1923–1982) a local writer, instructor, and community builder who became one of the most acclaimed American poets of his time. The center advances Hugo's vision by bringing innovative and effective writing programs and workshop education to people of all ages and backgrounds. Visitors are welcome to tour the 16,206-sq-ft (1505-sq-m) Victorian house, built in 1902. *Map E4 • 1634 11th Ave • (206) 322-7030 • Open 9am–6pm*

Seattle Pride March

What began as a protest in 1970 to commemorate the first anniversary of the Stonewall Riots in New York (which sparked the modern gay rights movement), has become a day of unbridled celebration, outlandish pageantry, music, and politicizing. Although Capitol Hill can no longer accommodate the large numbers that come to participate – the rally now takes place in Seattle Center – the Hill remains an important meeting place for Seattle's gay community.

Volunteer Park Observation Tower

7 Volunteer Park Observation Tower

Built by Seattle's water department in 1906, this 75-ft (23-m) brick tower with an observation deck was designed by the Olmsted Brothers. A short climb of 106 spiraling steps to the deck offers spectacular views of Puget Sound, the Space Needle, and the Olympic Mountains. Volunteer Park is also the site of the Seattle Asian Art Museum *(see p36)* and the Volunteer Park Conservatory. *Map E4*

8 Lake View Cemetery

This 1887-era cemetery, on a hilltop just past the northern end of Volunteer Park, is the final resting place for prominent Seattleites, and attracts thousands of visitors each year. Tombstones here identify the pioneers whose names now grace present-day streets or area towns – Denny, Maynard, Boren, Mercer, Yesler, and Renton. Lake View also draws the faithful followers of cinema star and martial arts master, Bruce Lee *(see p31)*, and his son Brandon, whose sculpted tombstones lie side by side. *Map E3 • 1554 15th E • (206) 322-1582*

If you're in Volunteer Park, plant lovers should check out the Volunteer Park Conservatory. Call (206) 684-4743 for information.

9 Neighborhood Homes

Stroll down the 3-block stretch of Denny between Broadway and Olive Way to scout for charming Victorian and Craftsman-style homes and elegant balconies decorated with hanging flower baskets or off-beat art. Marvel at the opulent mansions on the blocks just south of Volunteer Park. Capitol Hill's adjacent Central District, south of Madison and north of 14th Avenue East, is a transitional neighborhood but features view properties with gorgeous old homes – best seen by car.

10 Eastlake

An entire neighborhood disappeared when Interstate-5 cut a trough at the base of Capitol Hill. The sliver of a community that remains is called Eastlake, named after the main thoroughfare. Today, it survives as a mixed-use residential community at Lake Union's edge, popular with students, artists, and water-lovers as exemplified by the community of houseboats. REI's flagship store *(see p44)* marks the beginning of Eastlake's commercial area, and farther north, the neighborhood opens up with taverns, cafés, and stores that revel in the geography – halfway between downtown and the University District. *Map E3*

Neighborhood home, Denny Way

Up Pine Down Pike

Morning

Begin your late morning promenade at the corner of Pine and Melrose with a strong coffee at **Bauhaus Books & Coffee** *(see p75)*, a long-time Capitol Hill hangout. Walk along Pine (slightly uphill towards Broadway) but don't pass up **Vintage Chick** next door to Bauhaus for used duds with an edge. **Area 51** (401 E Pine St) is a huge space filled with vintage furniture and kitschy one-of-a-kinds. One block farther east lies **Linda's Tavern** *(see p75)*, a legendary local watering hole frequented by musicians and record label folk that you can scope out for a later visit. Cross Harvard Avenue and you'll notice the vintage **Egyptian Theater** *(see p39)* on your right, showcasing independent and foreign films.

Afternoon

Cross Broadway, walk four blocks, and turn right on 13th Avenue to Pike Street. Turn right and have lunch at **Elysian Brewery** *(see p49)*, home of Seattle's most outstanding pale ale. Walk downhill on Pike to the **Comet** (922 E Pike St), a grungy tavern that's popular with local musicians and wannabes. Cross Broadway and dream about a purchase at **Phil Smart's** (600 E Pike) for your gold-trimmed imported sports car, or stop by the **Seattle LGBT Community Center** *(see p74)*, a gay and lesbian information and activity center. Check in with those far away at **Uncle Elizabeth's Internet Café** (1123 Pike St), as downtown's skyline slips into view two blocks away.

Left **Wildrose** Center **Babeland** Right **Manray**

Top 10 Gay, Lesbian, Bisexual & Transgendered Venues

1 Neighbors

Witness hedonism at its best, with talent shows, wet 'n' wild contests, open mike nights, CD release parties, nightly drink specials, and dancing boys. Thursdays–Saturdays the club stays open for after hours dancing. *Map M3 • 1509 Broadway*

2 Wildrose

A lesbian-centric club, although it encourages a mixed and permissive crowd to assemble. The drinks are on the strong side. *Map M3 • 1021 E Pike*

3 Re-Bar

The entrance sign perhaps best sums up the philosophy of a club that features some of the area's best DJs: "No minors, drunks, drugs, bigots, or loudmouths." *Map L3 • 1114 Howell St*

4 Manray

It's been billed as a video bar, but the clientele arrives to look and be looked at. They serve stiff but pricey martinis. *Map L3 • 514 E Pine*

5 R Place

Capitol Hill's largest gay club has a full bar and music video monitors on its first floor; dart boards, free pool, and pinball on its second floor; and dancing, live DJs, karaoke, and a weekly strip show on its third floor. *Map L3 • 619 E Pine St*

6 Eagle

It's Seattle's oldest leather bar, and the atmosphere reeks of a crowd driven by studs and black leather straps and hard rock music. *Map L3 • 314 E Pike*

7 The Cuff Complex

An exclusive gay men's club catering to a crowd ranging from 20-somethings to middle agers. Arrive on Sundays for a kegger blowout. *Map M3 • 1533 13th Ave*

8 Lambert House Gay Youth Center

Organizes activities, support groups, a youth leadership council, dances, and other events to inspire empowerment among 14–22 year olds. The center includes a full kitchen, living room, pool table, library, TV, games, and most important, people who will listen. *Map E3 • 1818 15th Ave E*

9 Babeland

A store selling sex toys, and sponsoring a variety of sex workshops that continue to enlighten, amuse, and shock audiences. *Map L3 • 707 E Pike St • (206) 328-2914*

10 Seattle LGBT Community Center

This facility serves as the hub for Capitol Hill's gay and lesbian community. A great resource for activities and information. *Map L3 • 1115 E Pike St • (206) 323-5428*

Seattle is one of the most tolerant and liberal cities in the country, and its large gay population compares with San Francisco's.

Price Categories

Price categories include a three-course meal for one, two glasses of wine and all unavoidable extra charges including tax

$	under $20
$$	$20–$40
$$$	$40–$55
$$$$	$55–$80
$$$$$	over $80

Left **Bauhaus Books & Coffee** Right **Elysian Brewery sign**

TOP 10 Cafés & Taverns

1 Victrola
A real neighborhood café that roasts its own coffee in-house using beans from small farms. The aesthetics reflect music and art of the 1920s and 30s. *Map E4 • 411 15th Ave E • $*

2 Bauhaus Books & Coffee
They roast their own coffee here. Drink while you savor the delicious doughnuts and croissants. *Map L3 • 301 E Pine St • (206) 625-1600 • $*

3 B&O Espresso
A more refined and higher priced outlet for fine baked goods and specialty coffees. They also make deluxe wedding cakes and have a full service bistro next door. *Map L2 • 204 Belmont Ave E • (206) 322-5028 • $*

4 Espresso Vivace Roasteria
Their roasting process and promotion of caffe espresso as a culinary art has been well appreciated. The owners have published a book and two videos about the art that enjoys worldwide distribution. *Map M2 • 901 E Denny Way • $*

5 Coffee Messiah
In a city that has turned coffee retailers into millionaires, this tiny café began as a non-profit enterprise. Wireless internet access is available. *Map E4 • 1554 E Olive Way • $*

6 Chop Suey
(see p48)

7 Linda's Tavern
Linda Derschang, a local business owner, created a hip bar for locals in 1994 that tended at the time to be rock stars and their managers. Offers mixed drinks and beer, and decent food. *Map L3 • 707 E Pine St • $*

8 Bad Juju Lounge
DJs spin alternative music, rock, and whatever they feel like, and revelers take in New Orleans-style voodoo art. *Map M3 • 1425 10th Ave • $*

9 Comet Tavern
A legendary hangout for rockers and great pretenders alike. It's just a tavern with some pool tables, but the crowd, the location, and the stories etched into tabletops tell a different tale. *Map M3 • 922 E Pike St • $*

10 Elysian Brewery
The chow rates among the best pub grub in town *(see p49)*.

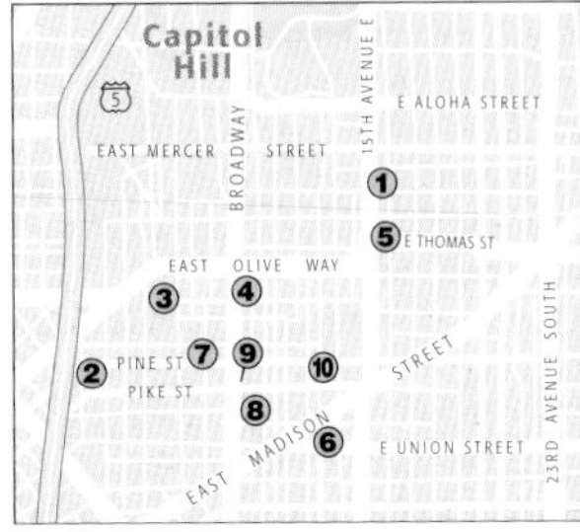

By law, bars and taverns check IDs to ensure that customers are 21 or older. Come prepared.

Chartreuse International

Top 10 Shops

1 Chartreuse International

The emphasis is on contemporary housewares and collectible 1950s furnishings by international designers such as Herman Miller, Starck, Alessi, and Eames. *Map L3 • 711 E Pike St*

2 Bailey/Coy Books

One of Seattle's smaller book retailers *(see pp18-19)* that specializes in gay and lesbian literature and periodicals. The staff is exceptionally well informed and friendly.

3 Edie's

Big spenders and frugal shoppers alike can shop for men's and women's footwear from chic manufacturers such as MOD, Camper, Aquatalia, and Diesel. *Map L3 • 319 E Pine St*

4 Value Village

This large thrift store is a Seattle original and has no pretension whatsoever. Items here are not necessarily fashionable, but they are always inexpensive. *Map M3 • 1525 11th Ave*

5 Lipstick Traces

The shop carries an assortment of designer-class merchandise such as toothbrushes from Italy, imported soaps and handbags, and novelty greeting cards. Most of the commodities are made locally, and the owner also sponsors art openings every first Thursday of the month. *Map L3 • 303 E Pine St*

6 Atlas Clothing

This trendy clothing store offers new and vintage wear along with shoes and accessories. Check out their array of colorful Adidas. *Map M3 • 1515 Broadway Ave E*

7 Martin-Zambito Gallery

Established in 1986, the art gallery specializes in 19th through 21st century American and early Northwest Regionalism, with special emphasis on contemporary figurative art, and early women artists. *Map L3 • 721 E Pike St*

8 Wall of Sound

A treasured small, independent shop selling new and used music CDs. Carries obscure recordings of rock, jazz, ethnic music, electronic, modern classical, and anything out of the ordinary. *Map L3 • 315 E Pine St*

9 Edge of the Circle

Seattle's resource for all things pagan and occult. Search for books on wicca, feng shui, neo-paganism, and santeria, or purchase your own tarot deck, goblets, and chalices. *Map L3 • 701 E Pike St*

10 Crypt Off Broadway

A bastion of fetish fashion since the 1980s, the store deals in the latest goth, punk, and industrial fashions. Also sells videos and other accessories. *Map M2 • 113 10th E*

Some stores will specially order an item not in stock, and ship it to you when it arrives.

Galerias

Price Categories

Price categories include a three-course meal for one, two glasses of wine and all unavoidable extra charges including tax

$	under $20
$$	$20–$40
$$$	$40–£55
$$$$	$55–$80
$$$$$	over $80

Top 10 Places to Eat

1 Galerias
For savory Mexican fare that's imaginatively prepared and not necessarily cheese heavy, this restaurant fits the bill with a wonderful decor and breezy room. *Map M1 • 611 E Broadway • (206) 322-5757 • $$*

2 Deluxe Bar & Grill
Serves an enviable list of brews and better-than-ordinary pub fare in the way of nachos, burgers, and salads. *Map M1 • 625 Broadway E • (206) 324-9697 • $*

3 Piroshki on Broadway
A tiny counter-wide place to grab perfectly rolled Eastern European style stuffed pastry. Choose from cases filled with steaming meat and vegetable piroshkis. *Map M2 • 128 Broadway E • (206) 322-2820 • $*

4 Annapurna Café
This family-run restaurant puts Nepalese, Indian, and Tibetan cuisine under one roof. Choose whichever dumpling, tandoori, or curry item sounds best. *Map M3 • 1833 Broadway • (206) 320-7770 • No wheelchair access • $*

5 Aoki
This longtime Broadway establishment rivals any sushi restaurant in town. Sit at the bar and watch your food being prepared or relax in Aoki's laid back dining room. *Map M1 • 621 Broadway E • (206) 324-3633 • $*

6 The Garage
Dodge the crowds at this fine dining, drinking, bowling, and pool-playing place with local rock star cred. *Map M4 • 1130 Broadway • (206) 322-2296 • $$*

7 Capitol Club
Fashionably aware 30-somethings, Mediterranean fare, plum-hued decor, and plush furnishings create the vibe at this popular spot. Strike it rich with the organic Kobe beef burger, a deluxe take on proletarian pride. *Map L3 • 414 E Pine St • (206) 325-2149 • $$*

8 HoneyHole
Find your way down Pike to this heartwarming source of Captiol Hill's hugest and most succulent sandwiches. *Map L3 • 703 E Pike St • (206) 709-1399 • $*

9 Bimbo's Bitchin' Burrito Kitchen
The alliterative name says it all, and everything here is a mouthful. *Map L3 • 506 E Pine St • (206) 329-9978 • $*

10 1200 Bistro
Outstanding cocktails and superb tasting plates. *Map M3 • 1200 E Pike St • (206) 320-1200 • $$*

Unless otherwise noted, all restaurants accept major credit cards and can accommodate vegetarians.

76

Left **Fremont mural** Right **Nouveau warehouse architecture**

Fremont

FREMONT DECLARED *itself an "artists' republic" in the 1960s, when a community of students, artists, and bohemians moved in, attracted by low rents. The name crystallizes the unflagging spirit of independence, eccentricity, and most of all, nonconformity. In retrospect, what may have begun as an idealistic artists' enclave was more accurately an early sign of fast advancing gentrification. The scenic Lake Washington Ship Canal and part of Lake Union create its southern border, and passing boats of all sizes continually refresh the view. The drawbridge on busy Fremont Avenue rises and falls deliriously umpteen times a day, snarling traffic that backs up the hill for blocks. The quaint neighborhood spawns new boutiques, clubs, and restaurants that keep changing the face and identity of this town. As Seattle grows and its population overflows, more and more professionals seek homes in Fremont, only minutes away from downtown by car or bus.*

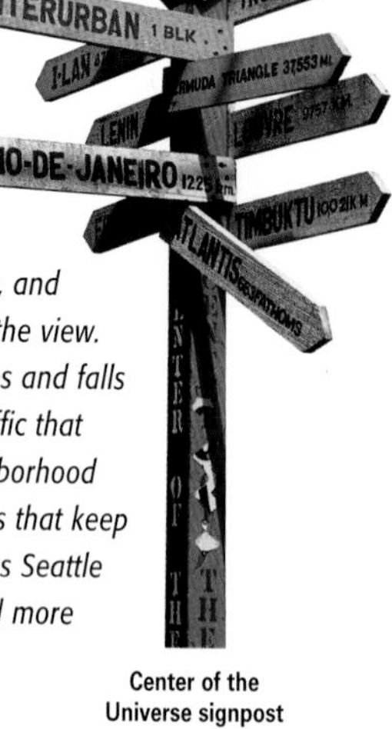

Center of the Universe signpost

Top 10 Sights

1. Fremont Bridge
2. Waiting for the Interurban
3. History House
4. Fremont Ferry
5. Lenin Statue
6. Dinosaur Topiaries
7. Fremont Troll
8. Ship Canal Park
9. Sunday Street Market
10. Outdoor Cinema

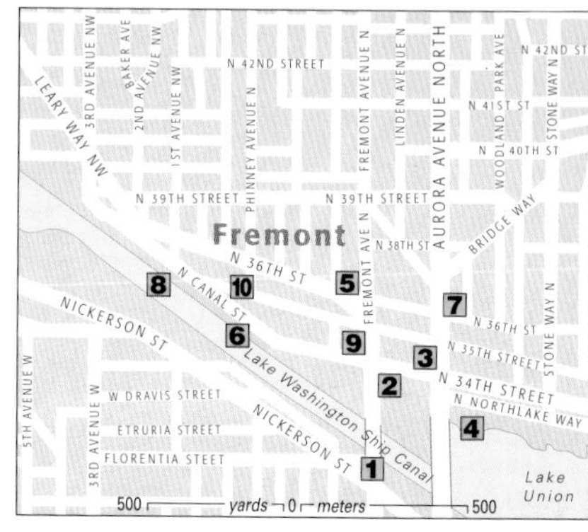

Previous pages **View of Mount Rainier and Lake Union**

1 Fremont Bridge

The lowest of four bridges spanning the Lake Washington Ship Canal, this connects Fremont to residential Queen Anne and two main arterials to downtown. Because of the bridge's low clearance, it faces frequent openings from sailboat, motor yacht, or industrial vessels. Neon art adorns a portion of the span, in the form of a golden-haired Rapunzel and her locks cascading down from the bridgeman's tower. *Map D3 • 3020 Westlake Ave N*

2 Waiting for the Interurban

Frozen in time, Richard Beyer's celebrated 1979 cast aluminum sculpture – five human forms and a dog with a human face – preside at Fremont's busiest intersection where a community trolley once stopped. Legend has it that the dog's likeness belongs to Arman Napoleon Stepanian, an activist-hero who sparked the recycling movement 30 years ago. The work pokes fun at modern humanity's ennui. It also

History House

represents one of Seattle's earliest public art installations. *Map D2 • N 34th St, Fremont Ave N*

3 History House

Seattle's colorful past is on view at History House where historians interpret and preserve the heritage of the city's distinct neighborhoods. Exhibits in the main gallery complement a three-sided, sepia-tone wall mural that depicts 100 years of Seattle history, encompassing the arts, technology, and industry. Peruse rotating displays of various Seattle neighborhoods. Other features include a sculpture garden and a gift shop. *Map D2 • 790 N 34th St • (206) 675-8875 • Adm $1 as donation • www.historyhouse.org*

People Waiting for the Interurban

The hype says Fremont's "funky," but renewed, remodeled, and retail is the trend.

4 Fremont Ferry

A boater's dream, the small passenger-only steamer plies the waters of Lake Union from its north shore in Fremont to the grounds along the southern shore near downtown during the July Wooden Boat Festival. A labor of love for captain, Larry Kezner, the ferry is strictly for sightseeing cruises along Seattle's Ship Canal and adjacent lakes. *Map D3 • (206) 713-8446 • SeattleFerrySvc@cs.com for private charters or schedule information*

5 Lenin Statue

Slovakian sculptor Emil Venkov found little interest in his 7-ton (6,350-kg), 25-ft (8-m) likeness of Russian revolutionary V.I. Lenin after the collapse of the Soviet Union. A visiting American, Lewis Carpenter, paid $13,000 for the work and had it shipped through the Panama Canal to his hometown near Seattle. After Carpenter died in 1994, Fremont artist and foundry owner Peter Bevis managed to have the bronze Lenin statue installed in the neighborhood. The incongruity of a Communist icon amidst flourishing shops and capitalist businesses is not lost on anyone. The statue remains a striking symbol that strives to put art before politics. *Map D2 • 3526 Fremont Avenue N*

Fremont Troll

6 Dinosaur Topiaries

Two ivy-covered dinosaur topiaries, which had formerly decorated the lawn near the Pacific Science Center *(see p11)* at Seattle Center, now grace Fremont's narrow Ship Canal Park. To save them from extinction, History House and a group of Fremont artists purchased these in 1999 for $1. The mother, 66-ft (20-m) long, and young apatosauri are now sanctioned by the city and fully integrated into the crazy quilt of what is virtually a neighborhood-wide sculpture garden. *Map D2 • Intersection of Phinney Ave & 34th*

7 Fremont Troll

An icon of Fremont's free spirit is a 15-ft (4.5-m) tall Volkswagen-eating troll created by Steve Badanes, Will Martin, Donna Walter, and Ross Whitehead, after winning a national competition sponsored by the Fremont Arts Council *(see p85)*, that in 1989 decided that public art was the best use for a dark space beneath a highway bridge. Though ugly, the troll's location under the north end of Aurora Bridge means that it remains on the route of almost every visitor who walks or takes a tour bus. *Map D2 • Intersection of Aurora Ave (Hwy 99) & N 36th St*

8 Ship Canal Park

A lovely landscaped strip not much wider than a stretch of the Burke-Gilman Trail *(see p84)* attracts tourists all year round. Today, the park creates view-points along the Canal and several places to sit, play chess, picnic, and watch the world go by. Pedestrians don't need to dodge speeding bicycles, however, since there is a separate gravel path for bi-peds. *Map C2 • Phinney Ave & 2nd Ave NW*

Although the professional class has moved in, Fremont's art community is still vital.

Sunday Street Market

9 Sunday Street Market

Rain or shine, the Fremont Sunday Market has withstood the test of time, real estate development, and even lawsuits from neighboring businesses. Begun in 1990 to foster a pedestrian-friendly community and provide an outlet for artists and independent vendors to sell whatever they had to offer, the market hosts up to 200 booths of crafts, imported goods, furniture, food, and knick-knacks that defy description. *Map D2 • 34th St • (206) 781-6776 • Every Sunday • Open 10am–5pm • www.fremontmarket.com/fremont*

10 Outdoor Cinema

The *trompe d'oeuil* screen and curtains on a factory wall attract hundreds of attendees for campy feature films. It grew from a sparsely attended free affair to a popular summer weekend event that charges admission. Part old-fashioned American drive-in, part Fremont irreverence, people bring their own chairs or sofas and occasionally compete in film-related games between reels. The shows begin after sundown, but audiences begin arriving for the best seats by mid-afternoon. *Map D2 • Saturday: 35th & Phinney Ave; Friday: N 34th & Stoneway • (206) 781-4230 • $5 donation*

A Morning Around Fremont

Start your picnic with an espresso at **ETG** (3512 Fremont Place N). Cross at the crosswalk just outside the door to 35th Street, turning right to spy the neon-adorned Army surplus missile at 35th and Evanston Avenue N. Turn left on Evanston and walk a block to **PCC** (600 N 34th), an organic market where you can pick up a delicious carry-out lunch.

Turn left on Evanston for an unobstructed view of the **Ship Canal** and **Fremont Bridge**. Turn right along the Canal path, walk about a block until you see the **Dinosaur Topiaries** at the beginning of the **Ship Canal Park**, a great place for your waterfront picnic. Catacorner is a historic brick streetcar barn that once housed **Redhook** *(see p49)*, one of the first microbreweries in Seattle. Now, it's a gourmet chocolate factory. Enjoy the walk down the Canal path, perhaps spotting sailboats or kayakers. When you turn back, exit the park at the topiaries and continue along 35th Street. If you visit during the **Sunday Market**, you'll find blocks of vendors and lots of foot traffic. Continue three blocks to Fremont Avenue, by the Fremont Bridge and the sculpture, *Waiting for the Interurban* *(see p81)* on a traffic island across the street. Turn left on Fremont Avenue, and get your bearings at the Center of the Universe signpost a half block later on another traffic island where Fremont Place begins. Stop in **Simply Desserts** (3421 Fremont Ave N) for the richest treats in town.

Aimless walking can be an adventure in Fremont. You just never know who or what will turn the next corner.

Left **Fremont Bridge with Aurora Bridge towering over it** Right **Adobe Systems building**

TOP 10 Burke-Gilman Trail Features

1 Bridges

The Burke-Gilman Trail passes under the Fremont Bridge *(see p81)* and the Aurora Bridge. Both span the Ship Canal, although only the drawbridge opens for boat traffic.

2 Lake Washington Rowing Club

Both athletic teams and individuals hoist their racing shells into the flow from here. The club's non-profit activities also include training lessons for beginners. *Map D3 • 910 N Northlake Way*

3 Adobe Systems

A waterfront office building that was designed to leverage the look of Fremont's erstwhile industrial structures houses this software company. *Map D3 • 801 N 34th St • (206) 675-7000*

4 Waiting for the Interurban

(see p81)

5 The Rocket

When an Army surplus store closed in Belltown, its outside adornment ended up in the hands of Fremont sculptors and painters who renovated the World War II-era missile and placed it atop this store. *Map D2 • 35th & Evanston Ave N*

6 Rope Swing

Sunny days attract a crowd of rope swingers who get dunked near where Phinney Ave N meets the Canal. *Map D2*

7 Old Trolley Barn

This large brick warehouse used to house Seattle's early mass transit vehicles, the trolleys. Since then, the building has been a microbrewery, an event rental facility, and a gourmet chocolate factory. *Map D2 • 34th & Phinney Ave N*

8 Indoor Sun Shoppe

Huge plants decorate the front, and bright grow lights illuminate the interior of Seattle's favorite neighborhood home and garden store. *Map C2*

9 Dock Overlook

The fenced-in area with benches and a roof sits right on the water, making it perfect for sunsets and bird- and boat-watching. Distant views include Salmon Bay's dry-dock industry and the Olympic Mountains beyond to the west. *Map C2*

10 Gravel Plant

Mounds of gravel, asphalt, and conveyor belts make stark contrast with the solemnity and serenity of the water and parkland nearby. *Map C2*

The Rocket's lights used to blink as the engine belched smoke every 45 minutes. That mission was eventually aborted.

Fremont Coffee Company interior

Top 10 Fremont Culture

1 First Fridays Art Walk

On the first Friday of each month, art galleries organize self-guided art walks to local studios and establishments including the Fremont Foundry's Gallery, Fremont Coffee Co., and Black Lab. *Fremont Foundry's Gallery 154: Map C2, 154 N 35th • Fremont Coffee Co.: Map D2, 459 N 36th • Black Lab: Map C2, 4216 Leary Way • 6–9pm*

2 Trolloween

A masquerade parade begins its route near the Fremont Troll *(see p82)*. This take-off on Halloween ends at a bizarre masked ball with lightshows and live entertainment. *Map D2 • 36th St N under Aurora Ave*

3 Pumpkin Carving Contests

During Oktoberfest celebrations, Fremont's brew fest includes the hilarious chainsaw pumpkin carving competitions.

4 Moisture Festival

This new addition to the funky Fremont scene combines elements of Burlesque and carnival for two weeks in spring. Held at the old Hale's Brewery warehouse. *Map C2 • 4301 Leary Way NW • www.moisturefestival.com*

5 Living Room

The most tolerant venue for art openings, film, open mics, tea, or just lounging around with neighborhood youth. *Map D2 • 4301 Fremont Ave N*

6 Summer Nights

Throughout the warm summer months the Summer Nights concert series brings world-class music to an outdoor stage on Lake Union in GasWorks Park *(see p46)*. The series features artists renowned for their contributions to rock, blues, jazz, and folk music. *Map D3 • 2101 N Northlake Way • www.summernights.org*

7 Fremont Arts Council

Based in an elementary school's 1892-vintage power-house, this community organization supports creative expression and artists. *Map D2 • 3940 Fremont Ave N • (206) 547-7440*

8 ToST

This upscale venue offers a comfortably dark, nightclub ambience and serves fine wines and cocktails, along with guest musical performers. *Map D2 • 513 N 36th St • (206) 547-0240*

9 Glass Art

Dale Chihuly's *(see p36)* influence can be seen in glass studios such as Edge of Glass. *Edge of Glass: Map D2; 513 N 36th St*

10 Fremont Library

The city's smallest and most charming library draws the resident literati to spend hours here instead of purchasing the latest author's masterpiece online. *Map D2 • 731 N 35th St • (206) 684-4084*

Left **Bitters Co** Right **Deluxe Junk interior**

Top 10 Shops

1 Steve's Fremont News
Find newspapers from all around the globe or just peruse their stunning assortment of magazines. Located right by the Metro bus stop. *Map D2 • 3416 Fremont Ave N*

2 Dusty Strings
Since 1979, this musical instrument store has attracted players and fans of folk music looking for an Irish harp, fiddle, rare acoustic guitar, or a workshop on hammered dulcimers. *Map D2 • 3406 Fremont Ave N*

3 Frank & Dunya
This outlet carries an odd assortment of handmade home furnishings, jewelry, unusual switch plates and spinning lanterns, ceramic toothbrush holders, and intricately carved wooden furniture. *Map D2 • 3418 Fremont Ave N*

4 Sonic Boom
An independent showroom for new and used CDs that specializes in alternative rock music, it also carries a wide range of popular musical styles. *Map D2 • 3414 Fremont Ave N*

5 Les Amis
Window shoppers find it hard to resist the rustic charm of this women's boutique that stocks designer items by Rozae Nichols, Diane von Furstenburg, Nanette Lepore, and Trina Turk. *Map D2 • 3420 Evanston Ave N*

6 Frame Up
A simple framing shop which morphed into a lovely and sophisticated resource for one-of-a-kind gift items. *Map D2 • 3515 Fremont Ave N*

7 Deluxe Junk
A must-see for its proud inventory of Art Deco home furnishings, dinettes, and campy tableware, the strange and the sublime. Deluxe Junk ignores trends and focuses on filling several showrooms with kitschy items. *Map D2 • 3518 Fremont Place*

8 Fremont Place Books
A great local source for gay and lesbian literature, mysteries, politics, and insightful recommendations from a gracious staff. *Map D2 • 621 N 35th*

9 Enexile
This is the exclusive shop for Dogma, Enexile's handmade, artfully designed merchandise for fashionable men and women. Choose from floral jersey skirts, velvet military coats, and hats for the bold and stylish. *Map D2 • 611 N 35th • (206) 633-5771*

10 Bitters Co
The owners scour the Far East, Southeast Asia, and their own roster of Washington artists and designers to handpick crafts, home furnishings, and personal accessories. *Map D2 • 513 N 36th • (206) 632-0886*

Brad's Swingside Café

Price Categories

Price categories include a three-course meal for one, two glasses of wine and all unavoidable extra charges including tax

$	under $20
$$	$20–$40
$$$	$40–$55
$$$$	$55–$80
$$$$$	over $80

Top 10 Places to Eat

1 Costa's Opa
A mainstay of Greek dining, expect delicious preparations of authentic specialties such as moussaka, kabobs, and spanokopita. *Map D3 • 3400 Fremont Ave N • (206) 633-4141 • $*

2 Blue C Sushi
It's a kaiten-style sushi restaurant with a conveyor belt that delivers sushi and teriyaki dinners. Seaweed salad is a surprise hit. *Map D2 • 3411 Fremont Ave N • (206) 633-3411 • $*

3 Fremont Classic Pizzeria
Try the savory tortellini gorgonzola, wild mushroom risotto, or pizza de mare, the latter with prawns and squid. *Map D2 • 4307 Fremont Ave N • (206) 548-9411 • $$*

4 Brad's Swingside Café
Chef-owner Brad Inserra enhances his Italian cuisine with flavors and approaches from regional US cuisine. A seafood special might include Dungeness crab, Alaskan halibut, locally made sausage, and dishes prepared with exotic African spices. *Map D2 • 4212 Fremont Ave N • (206) 633-4057 • $$*

5 El Camino
The place for great Mexican preparations using ingredients such as duck, pork adobo, rock shrimp, fresh fish, and chipotle peppers. The margaritas are excellent. *Map D2 • 607 N 35th • (206) 632-7303 • $*

6 Red Door
Draws huge crowds for its microbrews and tastefully prepared pub food. The burgers, ribs, salads, and sandwiches are just great. *Map D2 • 3401 Evanston Ave N • (206) 547-7521 • $*

7 KwanJai
You cannot go wrong ordering off the specials board or the regular menu in this Thai restaurant. *Map D2 • 469 N 36th St • (206) 632-3656 • $*

8 Qazi's
One of the best purveyors of classic Indian cuisine that takes no short cuts. Try the vegetable koftas, lamb korma, tandoori chicken, and bharta dishes along with some garlic naan. *Map D2 • 473 N 36th St • (206) 632-3575 • $*

9 Tacos Guaymas
This Mexican restaurant offers freshly prepared traditional dishes like chile rellenos, quesadillas, and a salsa bar. *Map C2 • 100 N 36th • (206) 547-5110 • $*

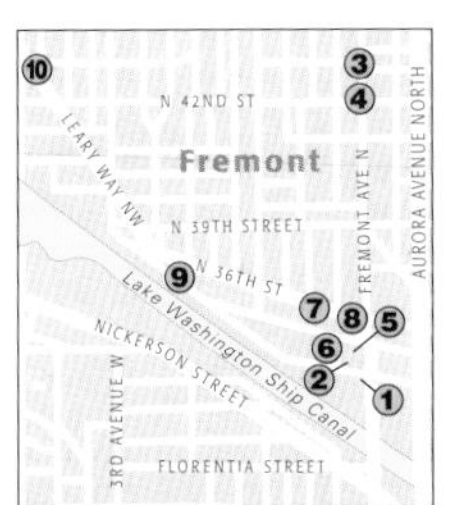

10 Hale's Brewery
Diners can sip the latest concoctions freshly brewed in one of Seattle's first authentic brewpubs *(see p49)*.

Unless otherwise noted, all restaurants accept major credit cards and can accommodate vegetarians.

Left **Old brick warehouses in Ballard** Right **Ballard docks**

Ballard

IN THE LATE 19TH CENTURY, Scandinavian loggers and fishermen established a working waterfront which is still functioning a full century later. Seattle annexed Ballard in 1907, taking advantage of the huge economic growth the mill town fostered; by then Ballard was the state's third largest city. Seattle's commercial fishing fleet resides at Fishermen's Terminal just across Salmon Bay. The late 1990s dot.com boom made real estate prices skyrocket, and scores of boutiques, art galleries, and restaurants opened, reflecting the changing demographics. Popular tourist attractions include the Hiram M. Chittenden Locks and Golden Gardens. The Nordic Heritage Museum celebrates the culture of the area's Scandinavian Americans, and every May 17, the annual Norwegian Constitution Day Parade takes over the streets.

Belltower, Ballard

Top 10 Sights

1. **Nordic Heritage Museum**
2. **Market Street**
3. **The Locks**
4. **Carl S. English, Jr. Botanical Gardens**
5. **Ballard Avenue**
6. **Golden Gardens**
7. **Fishermen's Terminal**
8. **Sunday's Farmer's Market**
9. **Bardahl Sign**
10. **Salmon Bay Industries**

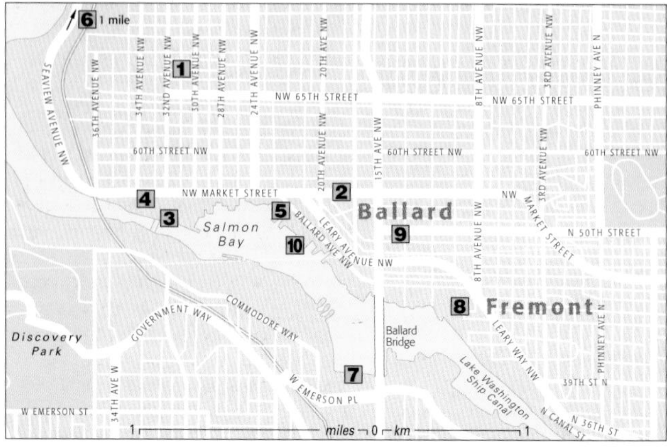

1 Nordic Heritage Museum

With rooms organized by country, this museum illustrates the links between Scandinavian people in the Pacific Northwest. Founded in 1980, it's the only museum in the United States to revere the legacy of immigrants from five Nordic countries – Denmark, Finland, Iceland, Norway, and Sweden. It also enlightens visitors with rotating and permanent exhibits such as colorful Old World textiles, rare china, books and bibles, woodworking tools, and carved wooden ale bowls. There is also a music library. *Map B1 • 3014 NW 67th St • Adm • www.nordicmuseum.org*

2 Market Street

The nerve center of Ballard has a vast selection of stores, cafés, Scandinavian gift shops, and taverns lining both sides of the street. Although Ballard is only about 4-miles (6-km) northwest of Pike Place Market *(see pp8-9)*, the street's melange of local businesses and creative signage reflects the community's small-town personality that has remained intact since the days before Ballard officially became part of Seattle. *Map B1*

Market Street

Salmon Waves, The Locks

3 The Locks

Every year, 100,000 vessels pass through the Ship Canal's Hiram M. Chittenden Locks *(see pp20– 21)*, and nearly as many tourists come to marvel at the site between Salmon Bay and Shilshole Bay. Named for a retired US Army Corps of Engineers general, the Locks' sophisticated engineering, and the sheer variety of pleasure boats and industrial ships that are able to pass through, impress visitors. The Locks also feature fish ladders to allow migrating salmon to leave from or return to their home streams, best observed between June and November. Don't miss the small but fascinating visitors' center, with its informative short film and displays. *Map B1 • Winter (Oct 1–Apr 30) 10am–4pm; Summer (May 1–Sep 30) 10am–6pm • The Army Corps of Engineers offer free guided tours Mar 1–Nov 30 • Visitors' center • (206) 783-7059 • 10am–4pm • Closed Tue–Wed*

4 Carl S. English, Jr. Botanical Gardens

Take a little time for a delightful promenade through the greenery of lush trees and rare and exotic plants that fill the garden's seven acres, bordering the Locks on the north side of the Ship Canal. The gift shop, which also serves visitors to the Locks, makes a guide available to assist in identifying the plants. *Map B1 • 3015 NW 54th St*

For in-depth information on the area, contact the Ballard Chamber of Commerce: (206) 784-9705, www.ballardchamber.com.

5 Ballard Avenue

From the roaring 1890s through the Great Depression, the four block stretch of brick-paved Ballard Avenue defines the *raison d'etre* of a mill town that also had a thriving boatbuilding and fishing industry. The 19th-century architecture is gorgeous, and it's easy to imagine a street filled with timber millworkers, salty fishermen, fishmongers, and the banks, saloons, and bordellos that served them. In 1976, Sweden's King Carl XVI Gustaf read the proclamation that identified Ballard Avenue as a National Historic District. *Map B1*

6 Golden Gardens

Ballard's largest park, and one of Seattle's true urban escapes, includes 87 acres of forested trails, beaches, picnic areas, and great views of Puget Sound and the Olympic Mountains. Originally, the gardens stood at the end of the line for electric streetcars which were funded by realtors, who wanted Seattle residents to get away from the city's noise and grit. Cool summer nights along the shore bring groups to huddle around bonfires, while sunny days see hundreds of revelers getting tans or playing volleyball in the sand. There is also an off-leash area for dogs, and a boat ramp at the marina. *See p47.*

Golden Gardens

Fishermen's Terminal

7 Fishermen's Terminal

The terminal provides moorage for more than 700 commercial fishing vessels and workboats. Because of the sheltered port and the area's supporting industries and businesses, many Northwest commercial fishermen regard Seattle as the best center for maintenance and repair. The bronze and stone Fishermen's Memorial sculpture, inscribed with the names of more than 500 local men and women, commemorates lives lost during the hard and dangerous work of fishing in Alaska. There are two seafood restaurants on the docks – one's a carry out with dockside tables. *Map C2 • 3919 18th Ave W*

8 Sunday's Farmer's Market

Like many neighborhoods in Seattle, Ballard attracts weekend shoppers by organizing regional farmers, artists, and craftspeople to fill closed-off streets with an Old World market. The lovely brick pavement and 19th-century architecture along Ballard Avenue form the backdrop for a pleasant walk for the visitors. The market operates year round, but when summer is in full swing, growers from the arid eastside of the Cascade Mountains bring their

Although Fishermen's Terminal lies across the Ship Canal from Ballard proper, it is integral to Ballard's identity.

bounty of organic produce, range fed chickens, and hormone-free beef to sell. Map C2

9 Bardahl Sign

Whether you travel by foot, bicycle, car, bus, boat, or plane, the towering, flashing, red neon advertisement for Bardahl automotive oil treatment makes for an unusual icon for any neighborhood. From distant hilltops, the sign's manic ascending flashes harken back to the industrial roots of Ballard, and to company founder Ole Bardahl, Ballard resident and Norwegian immigrant. The sign is one of Seattle's favorite, if most garish, urban landmarks. Map C1

Bardahl sign

10 Salmon Bay Industries

With the opening of the Sinclair Mill in the 1890s, Ballard was given the title "Shingle Capital of the World" as it was instrumental in rebuilding Seattle after the havoc wreaked by the Great Fire of 1889 *(see p30)*. Smaller firms and manufacturers, machine shops, and foundries settled in to stake their claims as well. Today, the area has not changed much. Skirting Ballard's southern waterfront along the Ship Canal, Salmon Bay industries include dry dock repair and maintenance for ocean-going container ships and barges, and a large gravel company whose equipment dominates the skyline. Map B2

A Morning Walk Down Ballard Avenue

Begin at the terminus of Ballard Avenue at **Market Street** *(see p89)*. Walk down the west side of the street. Get into gear at **Kavu** (5423 Ballard Ave), an independent retailer of active wear that's appropriate for dense woods or dinners out. Cross the street to **Marley's Snowboards** (5424 Ballard Ave NW) if you're considering a ski trip to the Cascade Mountains. Where 22nd Avenue meets Ballard Avenue is a large brick bell-tower, rebuilt from the original when Ballard's City Hall tower was destroyed by Seattle's devastating 1965 earthquake. At 5344 Ballard Avenue, **Olivine Atelier** entices with a luxurious boutique featuring local and European designer clothing and makeup. At the next intersection, you'll notice the highly stylized roof crest of what's now the **Starlight Hotel** (5300 Ballard Ave NW), which still has "Bank Building" across the top a full century later.

Cross the street. Look for **Tractor Tavern** *(see p48)*, a musical outlet for local and touring musicians who play jazz and country rock. **Second Ascent** (5209 Ballard Ave NW) specializes in clothing and gear for budget-minded fans of outdoor recreation. Find a remnant of days gone by at **Dock Street Brokers** (5101 Ballard Ave NW), whose signage matches the style of its century-old structure at 5109 Ballard Avenue. If you're hungry, turn back and stop in **The Other Coast Cafe** (5315 Ballard Ave NW) for East Coast-style sandwiches.

It's best to admire Ballard's industries from a distance. Waterfront car and truck traffic can be hazardous.

Left **Archie McPhee's** Right **Imagination Toys sign**

TOP 10 Shops

1 Turtle Press
Shop for hand-carved art stamps, hand-bound books and journals, tree-free and recycled decorative papers, and other artful tools perfect for inspiring creativity. The outlet also sells toys and gift items themed with its mascot, the turtle. *Map B1 • 2215 NW Market St*

2 Cookies
From edible adornments such as multicolored sprinkles to cutters and storage jars, this tiny store's shelves are fully stocked. It also sells the best chocolate-covered macaroons in town. *Map B1 • 2211 NW Market St*

3 Me 'n' Moms
This supply store for mothers and children sells cribs, consignment clothes, and imaginative toys at bargain prices. *Map B1 • 2821 NW Market St*

4 La Tienda Folk Art Gallery
Markets fine handmade crafts and artifacts from all over the world, including jewelry, ceramic bowls, carved wooden utensils, music, and instruments. *Map B1 • 2050 NW Market St*

5 Olsen's Scandinavian Foods
One of several Scandinavian import shops – this one specializing in their own smoked fish and homemade lutefisk – the traditional delicacy of cod soaked in lye. *Map B1 • 2205 NW Market*

6 Archie McPhee's
Call on the famous mail order gag gift company, which sells items in the rubber chicken category of humorous gifts. *Map B1 • 2428 NW Market St*

7 Metropolis III
This store has an enviable and loyal clientele of women in the age (or attitude) range of 25–55. The owner-operator specializes in updated contemporary fashions, using comfortable and versatile natural fabrics such as cotton and stain-resistant tencel. *Map B1 • 2318 NW Market St*

8 Imagination Toys
This store stocks plenty of kid stuff from entertaining and inspiring puzzles, spy and detective toys, to inexpensive novelties that are appropriate for gifts. *Map B1 • 2236 NW Market St*

9 Ballard Used & Rare Books
Have the staff search for an elusive out-of-print book, or browse the shelves for old but not forgotten favorites. *Map B1 • 2232 NW Market St*

10 Dandelion Botanical Company
Opened in 1996, this urban herbal apothecary stocks organic herbs, medicinal oils and tinctures, teas, and bath and body supplies. *Map B2 • 5424 Ballard Ave*

Order direct from Archie McPhee's fabulous funhouse website, www.mcphee.com

Delicious tempting naans

Price Categories

Price categories include a three-course meal for one, two glasses of wine and all unavoidable extra charges including tax.

$	under $20
$$	$20–$40
$$$	$40–$55
$$$$	$55–$80
$$$$$	over $80

TOP 10 Places to Eat

1 Lockspot Café
This eatery combines American staples at the busy take-out window with a bar and a restaurant inside. *Map B1 • 3005 NW 54th • (206) 789-4865 • $*

2 Ray's Boathouse & Café
(see p50)

3 Anthony's Homeport
Diners find excellent service, and fresh seafood that includes king salmon, Dungeness crab, and local oysters. *Map A1 • 6135 Seaview Ave NW • (206) 783-0780 • $$*

4 Le Gourmand
(see p51)

5 Burk's Café
Loyal clientele come here for Burk's southern cuisine, specifically Cajun and Creole styles. Order alder-smoked barbecue, jambalaya, or blackened rockfish to your heart's content. *Map B1 • 5411 Ballard Ave NW • (206) 782-0091 • $*

6 Hattie's Hat
A great source for huge breakfasts and American rib-sticking dinner standards with a twist: Guinness stout meatloaf, homemade creamed corn, sweet potato fries, and braised southern greens. *Map B1 • 5231 Ballard Ave NW • (206) 784-0175 • $*

7 Other Coast
Bridge the distance to New York City-style delicatessens by grabbing a sandwich here. Stick to basics such as the reuben with stone-ground mustard or the 12-inch meat or vegetarian subs. *Map B1 • 5315 Ballard Ave NW • (206) 789-0936 • $*

8 India Bistro
Relish meat and vegetarian plates prepared in North Indian style. Recommended dishes include spinach or mustard greens with paneer, spicy daal, succulent lamb or chicken tandoori and naan. *Map B1 • 2301 NW Market St • (206) 783-5080 • $$*

9 La Carta de Oaxaca
Beeline to this Mexican bistro with tremendous flair, and select from several entrees. The spartan decor is unusual, too – wall art consists of backlit photos of the region where all the flavors originate. *Map B1 • 5431 Ballard Ave NW • (206) 782-8722 • $*

10 Salmon Bay Café
This bastion of inexpensive eats attracts blue-collar workers and a large youth crowd. Great four-egg omelettes. *Map B2 • 5109 Shilshole Ave NW • (206) 782-5539 • Breakfast & lunch only • $*

Unless otherwise noted, all restaurants accept major credit cards and can accommodate vegetarians.

Left **Alki Bakery façade** Center **A coffee shop** Right **Sea stars**

West Seattle

A STRETCH OF ELLIOTT BAY *separates central Seattle from the peninsula of West Seattle, the city's oldest and largest district. Connected by a high freeway bridge and a lower span, West Seattle's proximity to both downtown and the Industrial District has always made it a popular residential area. More than 53,000 people reside here, for since the 1990s dot.com boom West Seattle has attracted an entirely new population of younger, entrepreneurial residents drawn by lower housing costs, the strong sense of community, and some of the best parklands in the city. Alki Beach and its paved waterfront trail bring hordes of revelers when the long, damp winter months give way to sunnier spring days.*

Bill Garnett's West Seattle Ferries mural depicting maritime industry

Top 10 Sights

1. **Alki Point**
2. **Constellation Beach**
3. **The Junction**
4. **West Seattle Bridge**
5. **Fauntleroy Ferry Terminal**
6. **Belvedere Park Viewpoint**
7. **Log House Museum**
8. **Camp Long**
9. **Walker Rock Garden**
10. **Steel Mill**

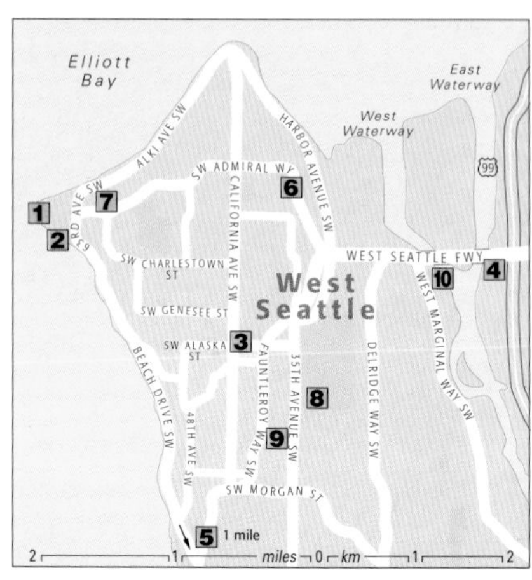

Previous pages **Walker Rock Garden**

Rollerbladers along Alki Beach

1 Alki Point

Seattle pioneer Arthur A. Denny *(see p30)* and his party aboard the ship *Exact* were the first Europeans to settle the region; they chose the beachhead of West Seattle to come ashore in 1851. Duwamish Tribe Chief Sealth *(see p31)* met the group with open arms and began a long friendship with Seattle's founders. Today, Alki Point boasts row after row of upscale waterfront condos for the well-to-do, and a great beach for shell hunting or scuba diving. *Map A5*

2 Constellation Beach

Seattle beachcombers check for the year's lowest tides and head to one of the best shoreline secrets, Constellation Beach. It's not the best recreational shore as it lacks a wide sandy stretch but gets its name from the large numbers of sea stars clinging to the rocky intertidal zone. If the conditions are right, it's not rare to find scores of colorful sea stars, along with the usual anemones, gargantuan sea snails, and geoducks, Puget Sound's giant clams. *Map A5*

3 The Junction

The Junction is the epicenter of what used to be an autonomous village in its own right. The name refers to the intersection where California Avenue and Alaska Street meet, and it is here that the bulk of West Seattle's restaurants and shops are located. The small- town feel is palpable as you stroll along California Avenue past mom 'n' pop shops and notice old-timers out for walks or sipping coffee at sidewalk tables. Murals painted on the sides of businesses mirror the warmth and pride of a tightly knit community in its prime, and reflect on its 150-year-old history. Illustrations include the original streetcar lines from 1918.
Map A6

4 West Seattle Bridge

From downtown, the fastest way to anywhere in West Seattle is via this highway, built in 1984. The bridge takes traffic from I-5 and other feeder streets over man-made Harbor Island and the mouth of the Duwamish River, and through to all the major streets in West Seattle. It's visible from many vantage points in town. *Map B5*

5 Fauntleroy Ferry Terminal

There's only one ferry from Seattle that gets you to pastoral Vashon Island, and that's the Fauntleroy Ferry with its terminal at the end of Fauntleroy Way. Unlike the downtown terminal, this one is in a residential neighborhood, adjacent to scenic Lincoln Park *(see p47)*. Allow some time to walk along the water's edge to watch ferries come and go. For a memorable visit to Vashon, bring a bike, and look into u-pick berry patches in summer months. *Map P3*

Some of the best views of mountains, water, and the city skyline originate from the hilltops in West Seattle.

6 **Belvedere Park Viewpoint**
For a bird's-eye view of the city of Seattle and its immediate environment, simply drive or take a bus up Admiral Way to tiny Belvedere Park. Take in 180-degree picture postcard views of the Cascade Range behind the high-rises of downtown, industrial Harbor Island and the Port of Seattle's container yards, and Elliott Bay and Puget Sound. On clear days, distant and permanently snow-capped Mount Baker on the northeastern horizon looms above all else. If you're in downtown, a 20-minute bus ride to Alki Beach drops you nearby on Olga Street SW. *Map B5 • 3600 Admiral Way SW*

7 **Log House Museum**
The museum, near Alki Beach, takes local history seriously, as it marks the location where Captain Folger steered his schooner *Exact* in 1851, and brought to the region the families of Seattle's earliest pioneers, the Arthur A. Denny party. The Log House Museum lets you rediscover the history of the Duwamish Peninsula with an orientation center and exhibits that preserve the community's legacy, speaker programs, and special events. *Map A5 • 3003 61st Avenue SW • (206) 938-5293 • Open on Thu noon–6pm, and weekends noon–3pm • Suggested donation: $2 (adult), $1 (child) • www.loghousemuseum.org*

8 **Camp Long**
In an entirely urban locale, Camp Long comes close to imparting the wild and natural experience usually found only during hikes in local mountain ranges. Once the 1941-era camp served only scouting organizations, but in 1984, the 68-acre compound opened to the general public. Inside the grounds, visitors can hike trails, learn about the environment from professional naturalists, or even rent rustic cabins for in-city camping. One of the most popular attractions is the 20-ft (6-m) high Schurman climbing rock, carefully designed to incorporate every climbing maneuver. Bats, Opossum, raccoons, chipmunks, and northern flying squirrels have been sighted in the camp. Weekly interpretive walks, rock climbing classes, and a golf course are also available. *Map B6 • 5200 35th SW • (206) 684-7434*

Golf course in Camp Long

Dredging the Duwamish

Before white settlers landed in what would become Seattle, the Duwamish River zigzagged throughout the valley between the hillsides of West Seattle and Beacon Hill to the east. The area was in many ways more wetland than river until the Army Corps of Engineers dredged it in the late 19th century, deepening the bed and making the Duwamish permanently navigable by commercial vessels. The dredge filled in tideflats to create Harbor Island, which lies between two small channels where the Duwamish pours into Elliott Bay. Many of the port's container yards and maritime industries use this advantageous depot acreage south of downtown.

Choose your activity based on weather conditions. If it's sunny and warm, head to Alki Beach or take a ferry ride.

9 Walker Rock Garden

Boeing worker Milton Walker failed in his task to create an ornamental concrete lake in his yard between 1959 and 1980. Never one to give up, he re-doubled his efforts to create an artistic vision that's outlived the builder. Walker devoted much of his time to sculpting towers, mini-mountains, and trails using countless sea shells, crystals, Brazilian agate, and colored glass. Today, the work remains on the private property still owned by his family. *Map B6 • 5407 37th SW • (206) 935-3036 • By appointment only, June through Labor Day*

Walker Rock Garden

10 Steel Mill

Seattle's remaining steel mill and the city's largest user of electrical power hunkers down on the Duwamish River's western shore. The mill processes recycled scrap from cans, cars, and construction materials just across the river from an upscale yacht marina and office park, embodying Seattle's ethic of mixed-use waterfront. While some may consider the plant an eyesore and major polluter, it competes successfully with Asian firms and provides jobs for the local economy. *Map B5*

A Morning at Alki Beach

Experience scenic Alki Avenue via an easy bike ride along a waterfront bike trail (about 3.5 flat miles each way). Begin at **Danny's Leather & Bikes** (3422 Harbor Ave SW) where you can rent beach bikes. Facing Danny's, head left. Near the 1100 block of Harbor Avenue, you'll notice **Don Armeni Park**, where wedding parties and professional photographers often congregate to snap pics of the city skyline. The road curves and becomes Alki Avenue, where you can take in great views with telescopes set up above the sea wall. **Public Restrooms** appear at the intersection of 57th Avenue SW. As you reach the central part of the beach community, Puget Sound and its ships and sailboats recede from view to the north, and the **Olympic Mountains** to the left.

At 60th Avenue, **Alki Beach Park** begins and supine bodies populate the sandy stretch. At 61st Avenue SW, look for the miniature **Statue of Liberty** on the right, built in 1952 on the strip of land early settlers had dubbed "New York Alki". At 63rd Avenue SW there's a monument erected to celebrate that landing party's arrival. Sweet tooths will get justifiably woozy at **Alki Bakery** *(see p101)*, and you can have lunch in the inhouse restaurant. As the street narrows and curves again, you'll see the **Coast Guard Station** (3201 Alki Ave), which offers tours of the Alki Point lighthouse on weekends from May to September.

Parking is extremely hard to find at Alki in summer. Consider taking a bus, biking, or walking from a short distance away.

Avalon Glass Works

Top 10 Shops

1 Avalon Glass Works
Find blown-glass vases, bowls, sculpture, ornaments, garden floats, paperweights, and seasonal items in myriad shapes, colors, and sizes in this exciting workshop. *Map B5 • 2914 SW Avalon Way*

2 Carmilia's
Along with assorted jewelry and accessories for women, the boutique sells apparel manufactured by Nanette Lepore, Ella Moss, and Hanky Panky. *Map A6 • 4528 California Ave SW*

3 Quid'nunc
The technical staff at this computer store are as friendly as they are savvy. You can buy software or hardware, or solve problems with whatever digital personal assistants you may have. *Map A6 • 4522 California Ave SW*

4 Admiral Metropolitan Market
This neighborhood supermarket and gourmet purveyor of prepared food offers customized salads, pasta dishes, and panini (grilled sandwiches) cooked to order, and creative side dishes galore. The store also sells quality kitchenware. *Map B5 • 2320 42nd Ave SW • $*

5 Morton's United
Professional and personalized service upholds the values of this small-town drug store. *Map A6 • 4707 California Ave SW*

6 Maggie's Cookbooks
The serious gourmand will need to save time to browse in the area's only bookseller dedicated to used and vintage cookbooks. *Map A6 • 6041 California Ave SW*

7 Easy Street Records
Shop here for the latest in Indie Rock then stop off for a spot of lunch and an espresso in the café. *Map A6 • 4559 California Ave SW*

8 Sweetie
Take your sweetie pie to Sweetie, for latest designer wear by such distinctive designers as Diane von Furstenberg, Rebecca Taylor, Wendy Hill, and Trina Turk. Impress your friends with a great selection of cool chandelier earrings, handbags, and belts. *Map A6 • 4508 California Ave SW*

9 Electric Train Shop
The eponymously named Electric Train Shop is Puget Sound's main depot for train aficionados. Stop in to relive your childhood memories. *Map A6 • 4511 California Ave SW*

10 JF Henry Kitchen & Tableware
This is the best resource for quality china, silver and stainless flatware, and crystal. The store carries hundreds of patterns displayed beautifully with great discount offers. *Map A6 • 4445 California Ave SW*

Browse Avalon Glass Studio's website for updates and a great selection of art glass for sale. Go to www.avalonglassworks.com

Luna Park interior

Price Categories

Price categories include a three-course meal for one, two glasses of wine and all unavoidable extra charges including tax.

$	under $20
$$	$20–$40
$$$	$40–$55
$$$$	$55–$80
$$$$$	over $80

Top 10 Places to Eat

1 La Rustica
Dine on exquisite Italian classics such as spaghetti with garlic, large prawns, polenta, or pizza with mushrooms and prosciutto. *Map A5 • 4100 Beach Drive SW • (206) 932-3020 • $$*

2 Alki Bakery
Specializes in decadently tall cakes, irresistible cookies, éclairs, berry pies, and cheesecakes. Also serves tasty salads, homemade soups, and sandwiches. *Map A5 • 2738 Alki Ave SW • (206) 935-1352 • $*

3 Luna Park
Inside, the decor and kitschy artifacts reflect the styles of the 1950s. Popular basics include the BLT and club sandwiches, hand-dipped malted milkshakes, and spinach salad. *Map B5 • 2918 SW Avalon Way • (206) 935-7250 • $*

4 Azuma Sushi
Insiders return often for their fix of professionally prepared sushi and sashimi, sake, and teriyaki at very reasonable prices. *Map A6 • 4533 California Ave SW • (206) 937-1148 • $*

5 Capers
A home furnishings and gift store with a sit-down café. Savor epicurean delights such as blackened breast of chicken Caesar salads, Moroccan stews, and sumptuous sandwiches on peasant bread. *Map A6 • 4521 California Ave SW • (206) 932-0371 • $*

6 Misto
A perfect bistro for fine espressos, grilled sandwiches, soups, and salads. *Map A6 • 4541 California Ave SW • (206) 935-8924 • $*

7 Jak's Grill
This steakhouse prepares the best beef, chicken, and fish dishes that are not only superbly done, but the price includes several side orders. *Map A6 • 4548 California Ave SW • (206) 937-7809 • $$*

8 Salty's on Alki
Specials reflect the freshest seasonal fish and seafood, and picture windows offer diners the most breathtaking views of Elliott Bay. *Map B5 • 1936 Harbor Ave SW • (206) 937-1600 • $$*

9 Chelan Café
Dine on typical American truck-stop fare; burgers, fries, meatloaf, or eggs. *Map B5 • 3527 Chelan Ave SW • (206) 932-7383 • $*

10 West 5
Munch on comfort food like BLTs and burgers at this hip eatery. *Map A6 • 4539 California Ave SW • (206) 937-1966 • $$*

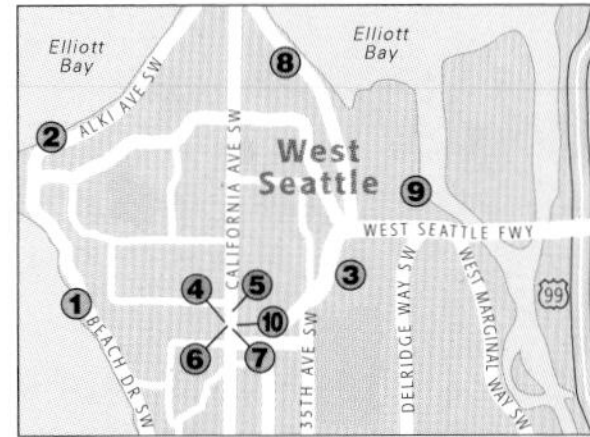

Following pages **Cafés on Pier 56, Elliott Bay**

ELLIOTTS

STREETSMART

Left **Seattle's Convention & Visitor's Bureau** Right **Maps**

Top 10 Planning Your Trip

1 Tourist Offices

Seattle's Convention & Visitor's Bureau can provide information for organizing a visit to Seattle, and Washington State Tourism is helpful for information on the rest of the state.

2 Media

Seattle has two major daily newspapers covering current events and vital information, the *Seattle Times* and *Seattle Post-Intelligencer*. The Thursday and Friday editions include special entertainment sections. Two public radio stations, KUOW (FM) and KEXP (FM), broadcast programs based on news and pop music.

3 Internet

Many Internet users have their own favorite travel sites, and the web has almost infinite resources for everyone. Websites with a wealth of information on Seattle include www.visitwashington.ws/seattle/bigpicture.html, seattleneighborhoods.com, www.lib.washington.edu/research/sea.html, and seattle.citysearch.com

4 Maps

Seattle's streets are arranged in a typical American-style grid. It's best to familiarize yourself with Seattle's layout, however, as bodies of water and steep hills create plenty of curves and cul-de-sacs. Pick up free maps at most tourist bureaus and attractions.

5 Insurance

It's wise, if not essential, to take out travel insurance before you travel. Policies can cover canceled flights or cruises and lost baggage in addition to medical expenses. If you have health insurance at home, save receipts from any medical expenses incurred during your trip.

6 When to Go

July is historically the driest month of the year, and late spring, summer, and early fall are the most mild and appealing times to visit. Most festivals and street fairs occur during the summer months. Be prepared for rain in fall, winter, and early spring.

7 What to Take

Seattle championed the informal look, so bring casual, all-purpose clothes. However, summer nights tend to cool down significantly, so a sweater or jacket is a necessity.

8 How Long to Stay

A week should allow plenty of time to take in the main attractions and to take a day trip or two. Two weeks would allow a more comprehensive experience in Seattle, as well as in its scenic outlying areas.

9 Visas

Canadian citizens must show proof of nationality in order to clear United States Customs. Japanese and most European citizens need a valid passport and a nonrefundable return ticket originating outside the United States to qualify for a 90-day visa. Other nationalities must secure a visa from a US consulate or embassy prior to travel.

10 Embassies

Every country has an official diplomatic representative from the United States. Contact the United States embassy or consulate in your country if you have any queries about visiting Seattle or current visa requirements.

Directory

Seattle's Convention & Visitor's Bureau
www.seeseattle.org

Washington State Tourism
www.experience washington.com

Seattle Times
http://seattletimes.nwsource.com

Seattle Post-Intelligencer
http://seattlepi.nwsource.com

KUOW 94.9 (FM)
www.kuow.org

KEXP 90.3 (FM)
www.kexp.org

For more information on embassies and consulates **See p111.**

Left **Seattle-Tacoma International Airport** Right **Amtrak**

Top 10 Getting To Seattle

1 Seattle-Tacoma International Airport

Sea-Tac Airport (SEA) lies about 10 miles (16 kms) south of Seattle. The main terminal leads out to the road where taxis and buses collect passengers. If you arrive at the north or south satellite terminals, you must first take a subway to the main terminal. *Map P3*

2 Customs

Federal law allows each visitor to bring in $100 worth of gifts, 1 liter of liquor, and 200 cigarettes duty-free. Cash or negotiable funds exceeding $10,000 must be declared.

3 Left Luggage

You may store your luggage at Ken's Baggage and Storage at Sea-Tac Airport on the Baggage Claim Level between Carousels 9 and 12.

4 Lost Property

Sea-Tac Airport operates a Lost and Found service in the central part of the Main Terminal. You can also contact your airline for items left on an airplane.

5 Shuttles & Buses

Shuttles stop at all major downtown hotels. The 194 bus is an express service to downtown. It costs $1.50; exact fare required. Check if your hotel reservation includes a free shuttle from the airport; otherwise look for Sea-Tac's Ground Transportation Information Booth or dial 55 from any Traveler's Information Board for information. Shuttle Express also offers shared ride service.

6 Taxi or Limousine

STITA is the only taxi company authorized to take passengers from the airport, although any carrier can bring you to the airport. Fares to downtown cost about $30 and take about 15 minutes, not including a suggested 10 percent tip. Private limousine services are more costly.

7 Portland International Airport (PDX)

Only a few miles outside of central Portland, Oregon, PDX is a distant alternative on the way to or from Seattle. It's possible to catch an Amtrak train to Seattle from Portland, sometimes for only $23 one way.

8 Kenmore Air

Visitors from Victoria or Vancouver, British Columbia, can make the memorable trip to Seattle on a seaplane that lands on Lake Union.

9 Greyhound

There are 4 buses everyday from San Francisco to Seattle, but the journey takes almost 24 hours.

10 Amtrak

Seattle's King Street Station is the depot for Amtrak passenger trains from Vancouver, British Columbia, and all points south and east. Find the entrance in between Pioneer Square and the International District. The Coast Starlight rides the rails between Los Angeles and Seattle daily, and Amtrak *Cascades* itineraries include towns and cities between Eugene, Oregon, and Vancouver, BC.

Directory

Airports

- *SEA: (206) 433-5388; www.seatac.org/seatac; lost+found@portseattle.org*
- *PDX: (877) 739-4636; www.flypdx.com*
- *Kenmore Air: 1-800-543-9595; www.kenmoreair.com*
- *Ken's Baggage & Storage: www.kensbaggage. com*

Bus

- *Greyhound Ticket Center: US; 1-800-229-9424, Canada; 1-800-661-8747, www.greyhound.com*

Train

- *King St Station: 1-800-872-7245, www.amtrak.com*

Shuttle

- *Shuttle Express: (425) 981-7000; www.shuttleexpress.com*

Metsker Maps of Seattle has a thorough inventory of maps. Call them at (206) 623-8747 or 1-800-727-4430

Left **A Seattle bus stop sign** Center **Seattle taxi cab** Right **Seaplane**

Top 10 Getting Around Seattle

1 Buses
Metro Transit offers the most inexpensive transportation. A single journey off-peak costs $1.25; peak times it's $1.50. Exact fare is required. Pay on entry for buses heading downtown, and on leaving for buses heading away from downtown. Ask the driver for a free transfer if you are connecting with another bus. There is a large Ride Free area downtown, where no fare is required. Most buses are equipped with wheelchair lifts.

2 Ferries
For a sensorial way to experience Seattle and its spectacular environs, consider taking a ferry. Major routes include: Seattle-Winslow (on Bainbridge Island) and Seattle-Bremerton from Pier 52; and West Seattle-Vashon Island and West Seattle-Southworth from the Fauntleroy terminal. From Anacortes, some distance north of Seattle, there is ferry service to the San Juan Islands and Sydney (on Vancouver Island, north of Victoria).

3 Water Taxis
The city has no water taxis per se but there are passenger-only ferries that bring commuters from Bremerton, on the Kitsap Peninsula. Occasionally water taxis run from Alki in West Seattle to the waterfront piers.

4 Taxis
Seattle has abundant licensed taxi operators, and you can flag them down from most downtown streets or call a cab by phone.

5 Seaplane
Kenmore Air *(see p105)* has a large fleet of seaplanes offering tours to sightsee Puget Sound, the Olympic Mountains, and the Cascade Range.

6 Car
Driving in Seattle can be a challenge due to large volumes of traffic on downtown streets, freeway logjams, and alternating one way streets that seem to baffle many drivers.

7 Boat
You can rent canoes and kayaks, or sailboats and fishing boats with or without crews. A number of companies on the waterfront, such as Argosy Tours and Spirit of Seattle, provide tours on Elliott Bay, Lake Union, and Lake Washington.

8 Motorbike
Motorbikes and gas or electric scooters provide more freedom and use far less fuel. Try renting one for an exciting way to explore Seattle's hilly terrain.

9 Bicycle
Cyclists are a lot safer on paths reserved exclusively for non-motorized vehicles. A city-wide bicycle helmet law took effect in 2004.

10 Commuter Rail
Seattle's commuter rail service, Sounder, links Seattle's King Street Station with Everett, Edmonds, Puyallup, Sumner, Auburn, Kent, Tukwila, and Tacoma. Service is quite limited, though; check schedules.

Directory

Buses
• *Metro Transit Rider Information: (206) 553-3000, (206) 287-8463; transit.metrokc.gov*

Ferry
• *Washington State Ferries: (206) 464-6400*

Car Rentals/Taxis
• *American Automobile Association: (206) 448-5353*

Motorbikes
• *Mountain to Sound Motorcycle Adventures: (425) 222-5598*

Bicycles
• *Gregg's Greenlake Cycle: (206) 523-1822* • *Alki Bicycle Company: (206) 938-3322* • *Maps: www.ci.seattle.wa.us/transportation/bikemaps.htm*

Commuter Rail
• *Sounder: 1-800-542-7876, 1-888-889-6368; www.soundtransit.org/sounder/sounder.htm*

Call Argosy Tours to see Seattle from the waterfront. Harbor cruises start at $18.25. Tel: (206) 623-1445

Left **Traffic sign for pedestrians** Center **No smoking sign** Right **Waterproof windbreaker**

Top 10 Things to Avoid

1 Don't Call it the Emerald City

This name derives from Seattle's rain-soaked greenery and once heavily forested ecology. But locals certainly do not refer to their home that way, although occasionally you may hear Seattle called Jet City, a reference to Boeing's influence on the economy.

2 Don't Jaywalk

Jaywalkers often find themselves collared by waiting police patrols on the lookout for any pedestrian crossing the street at unauthorized places or times. Police do enforce the statute that makes crossing against the light illegal.

3 Yield to Pedestrians

Seattle has a history of protecting pedestrians from collisions with automobiles. All motorized and self-powered vehicles riding the streets have an obligation to stop for pedestrians, whether or not they cross at intersections or outside of crosswalks.

4 Unsafe Neighborhoods

Most tourists never come near the edgier neighborhoods where economic disenfranchisement has helped to foster street crime. Seattle's major streets and arterials are quite safe for sightseeing during the day. Feel free to stroll at night only if you already know the area comfortably.

5 Smoking

Smoking is prohibited in all public places in Washington, including in hotels. As of December 2005 it is also an offence for smokers on the street to smoke within 25ft (7.6 m) of any doorway, window, or air vent. The 25ft rule is designed to prevent employees standing outside their place of work to smoke. Businesses caught violating the rule incur a $100 fine.

6 Driving Challenges

One's patience is tested when navigating Seattle's streets and highways. Keep a lookout for turn-only lanes at busy intersections. If you need to parallel park on steep hills, turn your wheels towards the curb to help prevent a runaway car. If you use manual transmission and you're stopped in traffic mid-hill, be sure to apply the emergency brake until you engage the gears smoothly. You must obey the speed limits, 25 mph (40 kmph), unless posted otherwise.

7 Underdressing

Seattle has two main seasons, wet and dry. Regardless of the time of year, always remember to pack a jacket or sweater, and basic rain gear. Waterproof windbreakers, hats, or polypropylene shells are essential.

8 Panhandlers & the Homeless

All cities have an abundance of homeless individuals, and Seattle is no exception. Avoid contact with panhandlers and beggars and those that are obviously intoxicated. They're rarely aggressive, but it's still a good idea to ignore confrontation. Always keep your possessions firmly in hand or secure.

9 Forgetting to Tip

Almost every restaurant's management keeps wages very low and expects customers' tips to make up the difference. Your gratuity should be in the 15 percent range, more or less depending on the quality of service, and calculated on the pre-tax total. Tip your cab driver 10-15 percent, and allow about $1 per service for hotel staff.

10 Age Restrictions & ID

The legal drinking age for alcoholic beverages is 21. The law is so strictly enforced that everyone's picture identity card is checked at bars and taverns regardless of how old they may look. Be prepared to show proof of age. You must be 18 or older in order to purchase cigarettes.

Parking meters downtown cost 25 cents for every 7 minutes. If you must drive, look for a parking garage or lot.

Left **Pike Place Market** Right **CityPass bus ticket**

Top 10 Budget Tips

1 Discount Air Tickets

You can uncover outstanding rates on the Internet. But be sure to call reservation numbers and search the websites of major airlines along with your forays into third-party travel sites to discover the most advantageous deals.

2 Hotel Deals

Hotel rates are subject to pricing grids based on such criteria as special promotions, high and low season rates, and room categories. Use your intuition; if something sounds impossibly low, it probably should not be trusted. Call the hotel directly and ask for the best price after researching wholesalers and even the hotel's own website *(see pp114–119)*.

3 Fly-Drive Packages

If you stay in or close to downtown and have no plans to explore the surrounding region, you will not need a car. But if you want to spread your wings, many fly-drive packages have built-in price advantages over renting a car separately.

4 Discount Coupons

Avoid waiting in long lines and get one universal pass online. You may purchase a CityPass online or at the first attraction you visit. It's good for nine days and includes admission to Woodland Park Zoo, the Space Needle, Pacific Science Center, Seattle Aquarium, the Museum of Flight, and Argosy Cruises. *www.seeseattle.org/coupons • www.citypass.net*

5 Cheaper Sleeps

The central location of Seattle's hostels combined with exceptionally low rates is too irresistible to ignore. Hostelling International, featuring a lounge, library, and self-service kitchen/laundry, and Green Tortoise Backpackers Hostel *(see p118)* are decent places to stay. *Hostelling International: Map J4 • 84 Union St • (206) 622-5443*

6 Cheaper Eateries

Cheap eats are widely available. Look anywhere in the International District, especially in the Vietnamese areas, for dinners under $7. Taquerias and sandwich delis dot corners in every neighborhood, and Indian restaurants offer all-you-can-eat lunch buffets.

7 Picnics

The Pike Place Market *(see pp8–9)* is a great place to shop for a picnic in one of the city's many parks. Try De-Laurenti's or Three Girl's Bakery for easily portable breads, sandwiches, salads, and freshly baked pastries. At Greenlake, purchase delicious organic carry-out food at PCC Natural Markets. *PCC Natural Markets: Map P2 • 7504 Aurora Ave N • (206) 525-3586*

8 Public Transport Passes

Seattle has no rapid transit system, but you can use the Metro bus system. For $5, the Metro Visitor Pass provides one day of unlimited travel to all major attractions. Or, purchase multiple ticket booklets of various dollar values. Call Metro Transit Rider Information *(see p106)*.

9 Communications

It may be a good idea to purchase a pre-paid phone card before you leave home. Most of Seattle's branch public libraries offer free Internet access at their computer stations. *Seattle Public Library: Map K5 • 1000 4th Ave • (206) 386-4636 • www.spl.org*

10 Laundromats

These have largely been relegated to lower income neighborhoods in a city that's on the expensive side. Maytag operates a coin-operated laundromat in the U-District. Check the yellow pages to see if there's one near where you're staying. *Maytag: Map E2 • 4522 Brooklyn NE • (206) 548-1321*

For information on discounted hotel rates within the city, check www.seeseattle.org/visitors/lodging

Left **Sign to help disabled travelers** Center **Braille Institute of Seattle** Right **Student's ID**

Top 10 Special Needs

1 Designated Parking
You may park in specially designated spaces if you are disabled and have the proper vehicle identification clearly posted. Any unauthorized use may cause a traffic infraction with a $250 penalty.
Department of Licensing: (306) 902-3770

2 Special Prices
Seattle's Metro Transit system and many other attractions offer discounted fare for senior citizens and the disabled. The Regional Reduced Fare Permit costs $3 and entitles you to reduced fares on Metro Transit, Washington State Ferries, Community Transit, and Sound Transit. Visitors wishing to obtain such a pass will need an American Disabilities Act (ADA) paratransit card. National parks also issue special vehicle passes for the disabled that entitle all passengers in the vehicle to enter for free.
ADA: (206) 553-3060 • Metro Rider Information: (206) 684-1739

3 Required Accessibility
Any new construction in Seattle must conform to the ADA by providing easy access for the disabled in wheelchairs. While newer hotels and restaurants will by law have met the requirements, you need to call in advance to inquire if your destination has conformed to the emerging standards.

4 "Kneeling" Buses
Seattle's Metro system pioneered the use of Lift-U lifts on public transportation buses to accommodate those who use wheelchairs or have difficulty using stairs. Look for a wheelchair symbol posted next to the scheduled arrival times on placards posted at bus stops.

5 Ramped Curbs
Every downtown corner provides ramped curbs, and frequent neighborhood street construction entails installing ramps where they do not already exist. Most government buildings, supermarkets, tourist attractions, performance venues, and hotels have clearly marked hands-free entrance and egress doorways and ramps.

6 Accessible Toilets
Seattle has an exemplary record of providing disabled access to toilets in public restrooms. However, public restrooms for the general public are few in Seattle, although there are public port-a-potties near the Pike Place Market.

7 Visually Impaired Travelers
Founded in 1965, the Community Services for the Blind and Partially Sighted is a great resource for sight-impaired individuals. The Seattle Public Library offers a Washington Talking Book & Braille Library and an equal access library program.
Community Services for the Blind & Partially Sighted: 1-800-458-4888; • Washington Talking Book & Braille Library: 1-800-542-0866, www.wtbbl.org

8 Gay & Lesbian Travelers
Seattle has many organizations that assist gay, lesbian, bisexual, and transgendered travelers with gender-related information.
Seattle LGBT Community Center: (206) 323-5428, www.seattlelgbt.org • Pride Foundation: (206) 323-3318, www.pridefoundation.org • PFLAG: (206) 325-7724, www.seattle-pflag.org • Lesbian Resource Center: (206) 322-3953, www.lrc.net • Lambert House (see p74)

9 Children's Needs
When traveling with children, be aware of their tired and sore feet, boredom, and short attention spans. Always pack a few snacks and essential medications.

10 Students
Use your student ID card for reduced admission to museums, festivals, gallery events, concerts, and other special programs.

Avoid downtown public restrooms as they are often havens for crime and/or unsanitary activity.

Left **An ATM** Center **US Post Office** Right **Coin-operated pay phone**

TOP 10 Banking & Communications

1 Exchange

Look for currency exchange offices in the Main Terminal and South Satellite at Sea-Tac Airport *(see p105)*, and at major banks downtown. Thomas Cook has an exchange branch at 4th Avenue and Pine as well. You can avoid bad rates by obtaining cash from ATMs, where daily rates are more advantageous.

2 ATMs

You may incur a small fee for using the ATM if you are not a customer of the bank (your own bank may charge you, too). Check with your bank for charge rates before you travel.

3 Credit Cards

Rental car agencies and hotels require a credit card for booking reservations. While many smaller eateries still do not accept cards, the majority of restaurants do. Call the bank's toll-free number if you lose your card. Always keep a small amount of cash for tips and small purchases.

4 Traveler's Checks

The use of debit and credit cards has made traveler's checks less popular. Their face value is equal to cash if you buy them in dollars, but you need to present a photo ID, and cashing them in banks or currency exchange offices can be time consuming.

5 Tax

Most restaurants charge 9.3 percent sales tax, while retail purchases are subject to a combined state and city sales tax of 8.6 percent. Car rentals at the airport include sales tax, an additional 10 percent tax, plus the 10 percent airport concession fee – 28.3 percent above initial rental price.

6 Post Offices

Most post offices operate Monday to Friday from 9am to 5pm; some branches open on Saturdays from 9am for 3–6 hours, depending on their location.

7 Telephones

Seattle's area code is 206, but the vastness of surrounding suburbs has necessitated several prefixes. 425 covers most of the Eastside *(see pp54–55)*, 253 covers south of the city, and 360 handles outlying areas. Local calls made from Seattle to those other areas require that you dial 1, the area code, and the seven-digit number. Toll-free numbers begin with 800, 877, or 888. Dial 411 for directory assistance, 011 for an international call, and 911 in case of an emergency.

8 Voice Mail

The novelty and convenience of voice mail has long since worn out its welcome. But it still has a vital place in both personal and professional realms. Leave your name, a brief message, and a call-back number if you expect positive results. The long beep is sometimes all you can count on hearing – especially if you are trying to make dinner reservations.

9 Internet

There's no shortage of Internet cafés in Seattle, and quite a few feature Wifi service for seamless remote and wireless connections laptop users. Charges vary, and occasionally there is no charge. Seattle public libraries *(see p108)* offer free Internet access, though time limits apply.

10 Courier Services

The most popular overnight mailing services are FedEx, UPS, and DHL. Also consider using the competitively priced services of the United States Post Office for overnight, second-, or third-day guaranteed deliveries.

Directory

Thomas Cook
1-800-287-7362

Express & Courier Mail
- *FedEx: 1-800-463-3339*
- *UPS: 1-800-742-5877*
- *DHL: 1-800-225-5345*

You may find the relatively rare $2 bill or a $1 coin in circulation in the US, but the former has virtually disappeared from use.

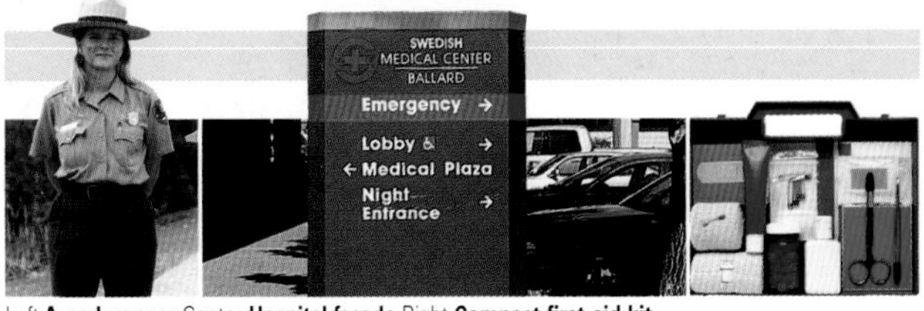

Left **A park ranger** Center **Hospital façade** Right **Compact first-aid kit**

Top 10 Security & Health

1 Earthquake Procedures

Should an earthquake strike, stay calm. If you are indoors, stand under a load-bearing door frame or get under a heavy desk or table. If you're driving, stay in the vehicle and park in an open area away from lamp posts and bridges. Major earthquakes are extremely rare, although the Puget Sound region includes several fault lines that are susceptible to temblors.

2 Consulates

Most major countries have consulates in the city. If anything untoward occurs, contact your national representative.

3 Petty Crime

Every city has problems with petty crime, especially for tourists who may look lost. The best defense is to be aware of your surroundings. Don't walk into any area that looks questionable.

4 Emergencies

Dial 911 from any phone during an emergency. Be prepared to provide your location and the circumstances to the aid dispatcher so that the appropriate help will arrive quickly.

5 AIDS

The AIDS virus is still a public health problem, so don't take risks of engaging in unprotected sex. Seattle has ample public health facilities and centers that offer free services.

6 Helplines

Find support and information for almost any problem via Seattle's public service helplines.

7 Police Reports

If you are the victim of a crime, you should report it to the nearest police department as soon as possible. You will be issued a police report, which will be needed for any insurance claims you make.

8 Outdoor Safety

Ask any staffer working at a reputable outdoor recreation store for general information about a particular area. Ranger stations are also excellent sources for information. Even for a day hike you'll want reserves of food, water, spare seasonal clothing, and first aid, among other personal items.

9 Hospitals & Clinics

Seattle has an enviable list of first-rate medical institutions that provide emergency care, health care services, and treatment, including Harborview Medical Center (Seattle's public hospital), Swedish Medical Center, and Virginia Mason Medical Center.

10 Health Insurance Claims

You should plan on paying for any health care at the time of (or even before receiving) treatment. Save receipts for reimbursement by your insurance company. Prevent billing worries by confirming in advance that the hospital or clinic you choose accepts your form of coverage.

Directory

Consulates

- *Australia: (206) 575-7446; austemb.org*
- *Canada: (206) 443-1372; www.usembassycanada.gov*
- *New Zealand: (360) 766-8002; ambnew@email.msn.com*
- *UK: (415) 617-1330; www.usembassy.org.uk*

AIDS

- *Washington State HIV/AIDS Hotline: 1-800-272-2437*

Helplines

- *Washington Poison Center: 800-222-1222*
- *Crisis Clinic: (206) 461-3222*
- *Rape Relief Crisis: (425) 252-4800*

Hospitals & Clinics

- *Harborview Medical Center: (206) 731-3000*
- *Swedish Medical Center: (206) 386-6000*
- *Virginia Mason Medical Center: (206) 223-6600*

Leave home with a clear understanding of how your health insurer handles payments and/or reimbursements.

Left **Sunday street market, Fremont** Right **Market Street, Ballard**

Top 10 Shopping Tips

1 Department Stores

Although suburban shopping malls have the bulk of nationally recognized chain department stores, downtown shopping opportunities serve the needs of Seattle's residents in a variety of ways. Find most of the larger stores, such as Nordstrom's flagship store and Bon-Macy, centered in the Westlake Plaza area between 4th and 5th Avenues and Pike and Stewart Streets *(see pp52–53)*.

2 Boutiques

Discover one-of-a-kind designer wear at dozens of independent clothiers that specialize in high-end fashion or more adventurous apparel with an edge. Several designers such as Carol McClellan, Darbury Stenderu, and Couture have their own shops in Belltown *(see p67)* and Fremont *(see p86)*, and many upscale boutiques dot the 5th Avenue area south of Pike Street.

3 Malls

As with most United States cities, large malls need the expansive and cheaper real estate found only in suburbs or outlying areas. However, there are smaller, somewhat pricey urban malls including Westlake Mall, Pacific Place, and Rainier Square *(see pp52–53)*. They also include familiar chain stores as well as locally owned ventures.

4 Flea Markets & Thrift Shops

If you like secondhand merchandise, you'll find bargains all over town. Many neighborhoods, including Ballard and Fremont, have outdoor farmer's markets on Sundays. There are also plenty of thrift shops; the best of these are Salvation Army, Value Village, and Seattle Goodwill, located on Capitol Hill and the ID. ® *Salvation Army: Map E6; 1010 4th Ave S • Value Village: Map M3; 1525 11th Ave • Seattle Goodwill: Map F6; Rainier Ave S & Dearborn St*

5 Garage & Sidewalk Sales

Walk or drive through any neighborhood on weekend mornings and you'll find a treasure trove of clothing, toys, furniture, and electronics up for sale. Look for large signs on telephone polls, or scour the newspaper classified ads to find appropriate listings.

6 Bargaining

Most consumers in the US shy away from bargaining tactics, but it really depends on the clerk, your powers of persuasion, and store policy. However, at flea markets and yard sales, it is common to negotiate for a better price.

7 Sales Tax

With the exception of groceries, all Seattle retail purchases are subject to combined state and city sales taxes of 8.6 percent.

8 Convenience Stores

It's relatively common to find a convenience store in commercial areas, even in exclusive neighborhoods. They sell a little bit of everything from fresh produce to deli items, snack food and drink, toiletries, and general supply merchandise. Remember you would pay considerably more than in supermarkets or drugstores.

9 Refunds

Always find out a store's policy on exchanging or returning items, or on obtaining credit. National chain stores often have a liberal return policy that may enable you to return goods at another branch once you're back at home.

10 Washington Attorney General's Office Public Inquiry Unit

If a retailer or service provider has dealt with you in an illegal fashion, do not hesitate to take your complaint here so that court proceedings can be initiated or sanctions be employed against the perpetrator. ® *1-800-551-4636*

For any unresolved complaints on a product you have purchased, call the Better Business Bureau at (206) 431-2222.

Left **Sushi** Center **Red wine** Right **Beer bottle labels**

TOP 10 Eating & Accommodation Tips

1 Pacific Rim Cuisine
In Seattle, this cuisine refers to fresh Pacific Northwest ingredients combined with the flavors and cooking techniques of countries bordering the Pacific Ocean. Chefs create masterpieces and signature dishes using sushi-grade fish, Kobe beef, ginger- and soy-based sauces, and handmade noodles to complement US menu mainstays.

2 Other Cuisines
You can hardly walk a block without meeting up with a Thai restaurant. Mexican taquerias compete with establishments serving Spanish tapas, while French and Italian bistros still attract crowds. Indian restaurants often include Pakistani, Tibetan, and Nepalese dishes as well.

3 Reservations
It's advisable to secure lunch or dinner reservations at formal or expensive restaurants, or at those with a view. Alternatively, consider dining at a non-peak hour, as getting a table anywhere special at noon or 6pm is a challenge.

4 Drinks
Washington has its share of award-winning vineyards. Better restaurants employ *sommeliers* to assist you in choosing wines to complement your meal, and they can also steer you toward a selection based on price. If beer or ale suits your taste, Washington has many microbreweries emulating the heavier British styles of ales and stouts, as well as crisp German lagers and Belgian Abbey ales.

5 Tax & Tipping
Restaurants add 9.3 percent sales tax to the total bill, and it's considered gracious if you leave a tip of at least 15 percent *(see p107)*.

6 Choosing Hotel Locations
For an urban experience or a central location, downtown is the hands-down pick. If you have a car or don't mind the distance, a number of B&Bs, boutique hotels, or guesthouses *(see pp114–119)* border the downtown area.

7 Hotel Gradings
All major hotels are subject to a widely accepted star-based system that gauges the overall merits, level of service, and amenities advertised by the property. Four-star hotels are the most luxurious and expensive. If you have any doubts, simply ask the reservation agent if the hotel has a rating. However, hotels rarely mention status unless they have a high score.

8 Making Hotel Reservations
Seattle has become a worldwide destination for huge conventions and large tour groups, many coming from cruise ships in the summer months when the tourist industry flourishes. Make your reservations in advance to avoid finding only a limited choice on arrival.

9 Extra Costs & Tipping
Occasionally, travel packages at downtown hotels include overnight parking with the room, but most charge exorbitant rates for the service. You are charged for making phones calls even when dialing a toll-free number. If the room includes a stocked refrigerator, anything consumed will add to the bill. Also remember to tip the housekeeper and other service providers at the hotel.

10 Traveling with Kids
Many hotels don't charge extra for kids 12 and under staying in their parents' room. Some have the same service for children 18 and under. Others may provide roll-away beds or cribs for a price. Search the neighborhood around Seattle Center for the most family-friendly hotels or motels. Parking lots nearby are often cheaper than the hotel's garage.

Taking home restaurant leftovers is not usually practical when you travel. Consider sharing meals or ordering small portions.

Left **Fairmont Olympic** Right **Edgewater Inn meeting room**

Top 10 Traditional Hotels

1 Westin

Located in two round towers, the Westin has an indoor pool, 24-hour room service, in-room movies, valet/laundry, two restaurants, a business center, and non-smoking rooms. *Map K3 • 1900 5th Ave • (206) 728-1000 • www.westin.com/seattle • Dis. access • $$*

2 Fairmont Olympic

One of Seattle's oldest four-star establishments, this landmark hotel has treated guests with the utmost elegance and personalized service since it opened in 1924. *Map K4 • 411 University St • 1-800-223-8772 • www.fairmont.com • Dis. access • $$$$*

3 Hilton

Its proximity to the Convention Center makes the Hilton popular with business travelers. All rooms are above the 14th floor, affording phenomenal views. Free HBO and cable TV, as well as such amenities as refrigerators, coffee makers, and hair dryers, are provided. Check out their senior citizen and family discount plans. *Map K4 • 1301 6th Ave • 1-800-426-0535 • www.seattlehilton.com • Dis. access • $$*

4 Sheraton

Guests can relax in front of the cozy lobby fireplace or head for The Gallery, a Northwest wine bar, for delicious hot and cold *hors d'oeuvres*, Washington state's award-winning wines, and a selection of fine cigars. *Map K4 • 1400 6th Ave • 1-800-325-3535 • www.sheraton.com/seattle • Dis. access • $$*

5 Grand Hyatt

This elegant hotel's deluxe rooms feature cordless, two-line phones and Internet access. Guests have free use of the sprawling health club, which has an exercise room, sauna, Jacuzzi, steam bath, lockers, circuit machines, and cardio machines with flat-screen televisions. *Map K3 • 721 Pine St • (206) 774-1234 • www.grandseattle.hyatt.com • Dis. access • $$$*

6 Renaissance Seattle

This deluxe hotel has a penthouse swimming pool, a whirlpool tub, and a workout room. It is near many major attractions *Map K5 • 515 Madison St • (206) 583-0300 • www.renaissanceseattle.com • Dis. access • $$$*

7 Seattle Marriott Waterfront

This waterfront gem with excellent views of Puget Sound and the Olympic Mountains opened in 2003 and is Seattle's first full-service hotel. Celebrity chef Todd English runs Fish Club inside this contemporary property. *Map H4 • 2100 Alaskan Way • (206) 443-5000 • www.seattlemarriottwaterfront.com • Dis. access • $$*

8 Edgewater Inn

All rooms combine luxury with Pacific Northwest charm. Features include handcrafted pine furniture, river rock fireplaces, Ralph Lauren bedding, turn-down service, deluxe bath amenities, and in-room Starbucks coffee service. A perfect alternative to downtown hotels. *Map H4 • 2411 Alaskan Way, Pier 67 • 1-800-624-0670 • www.edgewaterhotel.com • Dis. access • $$*

9 Courtyard (Westlake)

One of Marriott's less expensive hotels offers great lake views and proximity to Seattle Center and I-5. Rooms have free Internet access, and there's also an indoor swimming pool. *Map J1 • 925 Westlake Ave N • 1-800-321-2211 • www.courtyardlakeunion.com • Dis. access • $$*

10 Crowne Plaza

A reputed chain hotel with well-appointed rooms and an easy walk to the Convention Center and trendy boutiques. *Map K4 • 1113 6th Ave • 1-800-521-2762 • Dis. access • $$*

Unless otherwise stated, all traditional hotels accept credit cards, and have en-suite bathrooms and air conditioning.

Alexis hotel

Price Categories

For a standard, double room per night (with breakfast if included), taxes and extra charges	
$	under $100
$$	$100–200
$$$	$200–250
$$$$	$250–300
$$$$$	over $300

Top 10 Boutique Hotels

1 W

This sleek property attracts the hip, trendy, and well-heeled. It offers modern amenities, impeccable service, and signature ultra-comfortable beds. *Map K4 • 1112 4th Ave • (206) 264-6000 • www.whotels.com • Dis. access • $$$$*

2 Hotel Monaco

What was once a phone company's switching center is now a sophisticated hotel. All rooms come with a CD stereo. *Map K4 • 1101 4th Ave • 1-888-454-8397 • www.monaco-seattle.com • Dis. access • $$$*

3 Mayflower Park

Built in 1927, this is one of Seattle's last independently-owned hotels. Room designs reflect common Queen Anne touches in subtle and dark hues. The house restaurant is Andaluca, a small, top-rated establishment with excellent Mediterranean fare. The adjoining bar, Oliver's, makes exquisite martinis. *Map J4 • 405 Olive Way • 1-800-426-5100 • www.mayflowerpark.com • Dis. access • $$$*

4 Sorrento

At the opulent Sorrento guests find Seattle's finest luxury boutique hotel as well as a destination gourmet restaurant, the Hunt Club. Take pleasure in Italian marble bathrooms, 400 thread-count Egyptian cotton linens, and a complimentary car service within downtown. *Map L4 • 900 Madison St • 1-800-426-1265 • www.hotelsorrento.com • Dis. access • $$$$*

5 Alexis

Since 1901, the Alexis has lived up to its stellar reputation as an elegant haven for those who prefer pampering. Evening wine tasting, 24-hour room service, Internet access, steam and fitness room, full day spa, and the Bookstore Bar are some of the highlights. *Map K5 • 1007 1st Ave • 1-800-426-7033 • www.alexishotel.com • Dis. access • $$$*

6 Hotel Vintage Park

Part of the upscale Kimpton group, this hotel offers such comforts as plush terrycloth robes, lush fabrics and cherry wood furniture, and a hosted wine hour by a wood-burning fireplace in the lobby. Try Tulio, the award-winning Italian restaurant downstairs for a sumptuous dinner. *Map K4 • 1100 5th Ave • 1-800-624-4433 • www.hotelvintagepark.com • Dis. access • $$*

7 Roosevelt

This 1929-era hotel named for the 26th United States president is centrally located near downtown's best shopping centers. Evenings bring live jazz piano to the lobby, where the fireplace draws visitors to gather and relax. *Map K4 • 1531 7th Ave • 1-800-663-1144 • www.roosevelthotel.com • Dis. access • $$*

8 Hotel Max

Formerly the Vance, this hip boutique hotel features original artwork by local artists. Located in the heart of downtown. *Map K3 • 620 Stewart St • 1-866-833-6299 • www.hotelmaxseattle.com • Dis. access • $$*

9 Inn at Virginia Mason

Owned by the nearby Virginia Mason Hospital *(see p111)*, this 1920s-era inn entices visitors with wood-burning fireplaces in some rooms, a rooftop café, and excellent city views from residential Pill Hill. *Map L4 • 1006 Spring St • 1-800-283-6453 • Dis. access • $$*

10 Inn at Harbor Steps

This city-center hotel boasts amenities such as fireplaces, spa tubs, wet bar, and more. Rates include gourmet breakfast and afternoon *hors d'oeuvres*. There's also a fitness center, indoor pool, and basketball court. *Map J5 • 1221 1st Ave • 1-888-728-8910 • Dis. access • $$$*

Left **University Inn outdoor pool** Right **Watertown**

TOP 10 Neighborhood Hotels

1 Ace
This hotel, situated in a historic building, appeals to guests who prefer location over luxury. There are few amenities, instead the emphasis is on ultra-modern decor. Pike Place Market and the surrounding retail and art-infused Belltown are nearby. *Map H3 • 2423 1st Ave • (206) 448-4721 • www.acehotel.com • $$*

2 MarQueen Hotel
Queen Anne neighborhood's stately hotel provides a wonderful alternative to the area's chain motels and hotels. Walk to quaint cafés, trendy bars, and small shops. Reserve a room away from the street to avoid noise from the boisterous foot traffic heading to or from concerts and sports events. *Map G1 • 600 Queen Anne Ave N • 1-888-445-3076 • www.marqueen.com • Dis access • $$*

3 University Inn
Parents and students reserve early to save their spot at the University Inn, a non-smoking property located only three blocks from the University of Washington. Guests are treated to a free Continental breakfast and a courtesy shuttle to downtown. *Map E2 • 4140 Roosevelt Way NE • 1-800-733-3855 • www.universityinnseattle.com • Dis. access • $$*

4 Pioneer Square Hotel
History buffs and sports fans flock to this 19th-century landmark hotel featuring period decor and deluxe bathrooms. The bustling waterfront, ferry terminal, stadiums, and Pioneer Square historic district lie just outside. *Map K5 • 77 Yesler Way • 1-800-800-5514 • Dis. access • $$*

5 Inn at the Market
This inn pampers guests in an enviable locale with panoramic views of the Olympic Range and Mount Rainier. Consider dining at Campagne, the classic French restaurant, or its more casual country-style café. *Map J4 • 86 Pine St • 1-800-446-4484 • www.innatthemarket.com • Dis. access • $$$*

6 Inn at Queen Anne
Charm and a cozy ambience characterizes this 1930s-era inn. Rooms have kitchenettes and there's a plant-filled patio/courtyard on the property, perfect for sipping tea or coffee. *Map G2 • 505 1st Ave N • 1-800-952-5043 • www.innatqueenanne.com • Air conditioning for south-facing rooms • $$*

7 Silver Cloud Inn
This affordable Eastlake neighborhood inn provides complimentary breakfasts and shuttles to downtown. Many rooms have views of Lake Union and its seaplane traffic. *Map K1 • 1150 Fairview Ave N • 1-800-330-5812 • www.silvercloud.com • Dis. access • $$*

8 Seattle Hotel
You can get a real feel for downtown by staying at this inexpensive hotel, equidistant to such major attractions as Pioneer Square, Pike Place Market, and the Seattle Art Museum. *Map K4 • 315 Seneca St • 1-800-426-2439 • $$*

9 University Tower Hotel
An attractive choice for visiting parents, professors, and students, this award-winning hotel has 16 stories and designer rooms that offer comfy digs and great views of the U-District, the Space Needle, and the downtown skyline. *Map E2 • 4507 Brooklyn Ave NE • 1-800-899-0251 • www.meany.com • Dis. access • $$*

10 Watertown
Essentially a hotel catering to students and their parents, Watertown boasts non-smoking premises, complimentary breakfasts, loaner bicycles, and a free shuttle to select attractions. *Map E2 • 4242 Roosevelt Way NE • 1-866-944-4242 • www.watertownseattle.com • Dis. access • $$*

Be sure to check your hotel's cancellation policy. Some require 14 days advance notice if you change your mind.

Pensione Nichols

Price Categories

For a standard, double room per night (with breakfast if included), taxes and extra charges		
	$	under $100
	$$	$100–200
	$$$	$200–250
	$$$$	$250–300
	$$$$$	over $300

Top 10 B&Bs & Guesthouses

1 Pensione Nichols

Personalized services and its proximity to downtown make Pensione Nichols B&B a decent in-city choice. It may be a little worn on the edges, but the clear views of sparkling Puget Sound are great. *Map J4 • 1923 1st Ave • 1-800-440-7125 • No air conditioning • $*

2 Gaslight Inn

This lovingly restored 19th-century inn inspires guests with a notable private art collection. Highlights include a heated outdoor pool, fireplaces, stunning views, and Continental breakfast. *Map E4 • 1727 15th Ave • (206) 325-3654 • www.gaslight-inn.com • Some rooms have shared bath • No air conditioning • $*

3 Bed & Breakfast on Broadway

Located in a historical residential neighborhood north of the popular entertainment district, the features here include a parlor with grand piano, fireplace, Oriental rugs, antiques, and polished hardwood floors. Non-smoking. *Map L1 • 722 Broadway E • (206) 329-8933 • No air conditioning • $$*

4 11th Avenue Inn

This quiet neighborhood bed and breakfast is housed in a charming 1906 Victorian inn. The eight guestrooms are decorated with antique furnishings and boast modern amenities including wireless Internet access. All have queen beds and private bathrooms. Free on-site parking and dozens of local restaurants. Walking distance to downtown. *Map M3 • 121 11th Ave E • 1-800-370-8414 • www.11thavenueinn.com • No air conditioning • $$*

5 Bacon Mansion

This 1909 Edwardian Tudor mansion exudes elegance with original carved wood trim, 3,000-crystal chandelier, marble fireplaces, and a remarkable library. Most rooms have private baths. *Map E4 • 959 Broadway E • 1-800-240-1864 • Dis. access • No air conditioning • $$*

6 Salisbury House

Stay within walking distance of Volunteer Park and the Seattle Asian Art Museum at Salisbury House, built in 1904. Try the suite with a private entrance, fireplace, and Jacuzzi. *Map E4 • 750 16th Ave E • (206) 328-8682 • www.salisburyhouse.com • No air conditioning • $$*

7 Chelsea House Station

Built in 1929, this inn is tastefully decorated in Arts and Crafts furniture. All 9 rooms and suites offer private baths. It is located near Woodland Park Zoo; Metro buses stop 3 blocks away. *Map D2 • 4915 Linden Ave N • 1-800-400-6077 • www.bandbseattle.com • No air conditioning • $$*

8 Hill House B&B

Bask in an interior graced with settees covered in silk or tapestries, beveled windows draped with chintz swags, hardwood floors, and delightful Persian rugs in this 1903 Victorian inn. *Map M2 • 1113 East John St • 1-866-417-4455 • No air conditioning • $*

9 Mildred's B&B

This large, double-turreted 1890 Victorian inn brings guests back in time with lace curtains, red carpets, and a wrap-around front porch that's perfect for lounging. Across from Volunteer Park. *Map E4 • 1202 15th Ave E • 1-800-327-9692 • No air conditioning • $$*

10 Swallow's Nest Guest Cottages

A 15-minute ferry ride from West Seattle to Vashon Island *(see p56)* takes you to this hideway consisting of cottages in unique settings. Some feature wooded environs and also offer views of Mount Rainier and the island's quaint harbor. *Map N3 • 6030 248th St SW, Vashon/Maury Island • 1-800-269-6378 • www.vashonislandcottages.com • $*

Rooms in older homes and guesthouses may not have en-suite bathrooms or air conditioning.

Left **Travelodge Space Needle** Right **Green Tortoise Hostel**

Top 10 Budget Hotels & Hostels

1 King's Inn

The inn includes free parking with your nightly rate, and local and toll-free calls are gratis. Suites come with coffee maker, microwave, and a refrigerator. There's also a coin-op laundry on the premises. *Map J3 • 2106 5th Ave • (206) 441-8833 • $*

2 Travelodge Space Needle

Comfortable rooms, in-room coffee, and free local calls at this motel near the Space Needle. Amenities are few, but there is a children's play area, free Continental breakfast, an outdoor pool, and parking for guests. *Map J2 • 200 6th Ave N • (206) 441-7878 • Dis. access • $*

3 Days Inn Seattle Downtown

Unlike many budget hotels, this one has its own restaurant, the Greenhouse Café, which serves three hearty meals a day, and has a full bar and lounge. *Map J3 • 2205 7th Ave • (206) 448-3434 • www.daysinntowncenter.com • Dis. access • $*

4 Holiday Inn

Rates include a deluxe Continental breakfast, free covered parking, free local calls, two-line phones with data port, and an indoor pool and workout facility. Some rooms have a Jacuzzi. *Map J2 • 226 Aurora Ave N • (206) 441-7222 • www.hiexpress.com/sea-cityctr • Dis. access • $$*

5 Warwick Hotel

This hotel is a first-rate choice for travelers who want basic amenities at much lower prices. On top of many 24-hour extras such as room service, business and fitness center, and courtesy van for anywhere within 2 miles (3 km), there's also Internet access, and rooms trimmed in fine woods and Italian marble. *Map J3 • 401 Lenora St • 1-800-426-9280 • Dis. access • $$*

6 College Inn

Built for the 1909 Alaska-Yukon Exposition, this historic landmark inn offers old-world charm and hospitality. Rooms come with washbasin, mirror, and minimal furniture. Rates include Continental breakfast. *Map E2 • 4000 University Way NE • (206) 633-4441 • www.collegeinnseattle. com • $*

7 Vagabond Inn

Located on noisy Aurora Avenue, the Vagabond is convenient to Seattle Center. Start your day with a complimentary Continental breakfast and a swim in the pool. *Map J2 • 325 Aurora Ave N • 1-800-522-1555 • $*

8 Panama Hotel

Sabro Ozasa, a Japanese architect and graduate of the UW, built this hotel in 1910. Since then, it has housed Japanese immigrants, Alaskan fisherman, and international travelers. It is also home to the country's only remaining Japanese bathhouse *(sento)*; it's no longer in use, however. A multi-lingual staff is on hand to assist guests. The hotel also offers free wireless Internet access. *Map L6 • 605 S Main St • (206) 223-9242 • www.panamahotelseattle.com • No air conditioning • $*

9 Green Tortoise Hostel

Backpackers, students, and US travelers on the cheap frequent this hostel as its rates include free breakfast, Internet access, and retail discount card. *Map J4 • 105 Pike St • (206) 340-1222 • www.greentortoise.net • No air conditioning • $*

10 Seattle International Youth Hostel

This reputable hostel association's accommodations are simple and cheap. Guests can use the lounge, library, and self-service kitchen and laundry. *Map J4 • 84 Union St • 1-888-622-5443 • www.hiseattle.org • Dis. access • No air conditioning • $*

Find the best deals by calling the hotel's main toll-free reservation number.

Marvin Gardens Inn – Apartments

Price Categories

For a standard, double room per night (with breakfast if included), taxes and extra charges

$	under $100
$$	$100–200
$$$	$200–250
$$$$	$250–300
$$$$$	over $300

Top 10 Apartments & Private Homes

1 Accommodations Plus Inc.

Corporate clients as well as leisure travelers take advantage of this outfit's decent rates for fully furnished and comfortable rooms. Most Puget Sound-area apartments have fully-equipped kitchens, linens, plus all utilities and bi-weekly maid service. *1-888-925-0763 • www.aplusnw.com • $*

2 Greenlake Townhouse

For longer stays of a week or more, here's a charming home in the Greenlake neighborhood. There are three bedrooms, two baths, gas fireplace, two decks, cable TV, and Internet service. *Map E1 • 7407 4th Ave NE • (425) 744-1401 • Weekly rates from $1,200–$1,400*

3 Marvin Gardens Inn – Apartments

Consider a short- or long-term stay in the heart of Seattle in fully furnished studio apartments with kitchenettes. Premises include coin-op laundry, 24-hour front desk, and maid service. *Map J3 • 2301 3rd Ave • 1-800-443-3031 • www.marvingardens-inn.com • Dis. access • $745/month*

4 Sea to Sky Rentals

This property management company represents over thirty apartments, condos and homes throughout Seattle. Amenities include Internet access, parking, and the flexibility of daily, weekly, or monthly rates. *Map C2 • 4321 6th Avenue NW • 1-877-632-4210 • www.seatoskyrentals.com • $$*

5 Seattle Suites

Booking an affordable executive suite downtown provides an upscale alternative for families or individuals looking for unique accommodations. Each apartment is fully furnished, and many offer fabulous city views. Enjoy complimentary Starbucks coffee and a game room with a pool table and big screen TV. Weekly and monthly rates are available; minimum stays of three nights. *Map K4 • 1400 Hubbell Place #1103 • (206) 232-2799 • www.seattlesuite.com • $$*

6 Chambered Nautilus

This gracious 1915 Georgian Colonial home is close to the UW campus. Four rooms have porches overlooking gardens and mountains, and guests stay in nicely furnished one- or two-bedroom apartments. *Map F2 • 5005 22nd Ave NE • (206) 522-2536 • www.chamberednautilus.com • $$*

7 The Vermont Inn – Apartments

Modest, affordable, and comfortably furnished studio apartments with kitchenettes are on offer here. Features include a roof deck, exercise room, 24-hour front desk, and maid service. *Map H3 • 2721 4th Ave • 1-800-441-5805 • www.vermont-inn.com • Dis. access • $795/month*

8 Wikstrom Art Works

This light-filled guest apartment's unusual name derives from the owner's artistic pro-clivities and philosophical outlooks. The beautiful garden setting atop the Magnolia Hill is a real plus, and you can rent the space by the week or by the month. *Map B2 • 2807 W Bertona • (206) 283-0262 • $$*

9 Short Term Suites

Choose from furnished corporate suites in many favored Seattle neighborhoods, such as Queen Anne, Fremont, Capitol Hill, and First Hill. These accommodations are priced to fit every need and budget. *E-mail: Dale@ShortTermSuites.com • Lorna@ShortTermSuites. com • FAX: (206) 285-9502 or (206) 652-9356 • www.shorttermsuites.com • $$*

10 Home Exchange Inc.

Home exchangers simply trade their homes at a time that is convenient to both parties. *1-800-877-8723 or (310) 798-3864 • www.homeexchange.com*

Unless otherwise stated, all hotels accept credit cards, and have en-suite bathrooms and air conditioning.

General Index

Index

Acknowledgements

The Author
Eric Amrine is a freelance writer and musician living with his wife and two children in Seattle's Fremont district. His favorite travel assignments include hiking, kayaking, and wildlife, and have taken him through Alaska's Inside Passage via luxury yacht, white-water rafting in Oregon's Rogue River wilderness, and expedition cruising to pristine beaches and remote islands of the Sea of Cortez, Mexico.

Photographer Frank L. Jenkins
The photographer would like to thank Anna Webster for her assistance and help

Additional Photography
Max Alexander, Andy Crawford, Philip Gatward, Heidi Grassley, Frank Greenaway, Dave King, Eddie Lawrence, Gunter Marx, Andrew McKinney, David Murray, Ian O'Leary, Scott Pitts, Guy Ryecart, Chris Stowers, Clive Streeter, Linda Whitwam, Francesca Yorke

AT DK INDIA:
Managing Editor Aruna Ghose
Art Editor Benu Joshi
Project Editor Vandana Bhagra
Project Designers Bonita Vaz, Divya Saxena
Senior Cartographer Uma Bhattacharya
Cartographer Alok Pathak
Picture Researcher Taiyaba Khatoon
Fact Checker Paul Townsend
Indexer & Proofreader Bhavna Seth Ranjan
DTP Co-ordinator Shailesh Sharma
DTP Designer Vinod Harish

AT DK LONDON:
Publishing Manager Helen Townsend
Managing Art Editor Jane Ewart
Senior Cartographic Editor Casper Morris
Senior DTP Designer Jason Little
DK Picture Library Romaine Werblow, Hayley Smith, Gemma Woodward
Production Linda Dare

Additional contributors Anna Freiberger, Eric Houghton, Sangita Patel, Marianne Petrou, Ros Walford

Picture Credits
t-top, tl-top left; tlc-top left centre; tc-top centre; tr-top right; cla-centre left above; ca-centre above; cra-centre right above; cl-centre left; c-centre; cr-centre right; clb-centre left below; cb-centre below; crb-centre right below; bl-bottom left, b-bottom; bc-bottom centre; bcl-bottom centre left; br-bottom right; d-detail.

Every effort has been made to trace the copyright holders of images, and we apologize in advance for any unintentional omissions. We would be pleased to insert the appropriate acknowledgements in any subsequent edition of this publication.

The publisher would also like to thank the following for their assistance and kind permission to photograph at their establishments: Guitar Gallery at Experience Music Project, located in Seattle, Washington; Klondike Gold Rush National Historic Park; Pacific Place Shopping Center;

Seattle Art Museum; Seattle Children's Museum; Smith Tower.

Works of art have been reproduced with the permission of the following copyright holders: Georgia Gerber *Rachel the Market Pig* 2tl, 62cl; Jonathan Borofsky *Hammering Man* 3br, 36ca, 36tl; Seattle Public Utilities *Decorative Manhole Cover* 6bl; Jack Mackie *Dance Steps on Broadway* 1981 18b; Richard Beyer *People Waiting for the Interurban* 81b; Steve Badanes, Will Martin, Donna Walter and Ross Whitehead *Fremont Troll* 1990 82bl; Paul Sorey *Salmon Waves* 2001 89tr; Bill Garnett *West Seattle Ferries 96c*.

The publishers would like to thank the following individuals, companies and picture libraries for their kind permission to reproduce their photographs.

ALAMY: Brad Mitchell 4-5; Chuck Pefley 3bl, 21tl, 27tl, 78-79; Picturenet Corporation 10-11c; Robert Harding World Imagery 102-103.

BABELAND: Audrey McManus 74tc; THE BERGER PARTNERSHIP: The interactive water feature (sculpture) at Cal Anderson Park was a result of a collaborative effort between artist Doug Hollis and the landscape architect The Berger Partnership photo Doug Hollis 18-19; BITTERS CO.: Linda Ferrol 86tl.

CORBIS: Morton Beebe 34 tr; Richard Cummins 12-13c; Henry Diltz 31tr; Ric Ergenbright 22-23c; Kelly Mooney Photography 26-27c; Museum of History and Industry 30c; Douglas Peebles 6br, 35tr; Neil Rabinowitz 20-21c, 34tl, 34cl; Joel W. Rogers 9b; Museum of History and Industry/ © Seattle Post-Intelligencer Collection 37tr; Robert Sorbo 31tl; Paul A. Souders 60-61; Jay Syverson 16-17c; Karl Weatherly 28-29; Webster & Stevens Collection Seattle 30tl.

EDGEWATER INN: 114tr.

FAIRMONT OLYMPIC: 114tl.

MANRAY VIDEO BAR: 74tr.

SEATTLE CONVENTION & VISITORS BUREAU: Daryl Smith *Jimi Hendrix Statue* photo David Blanchford 18tr; SEATTLE PHOTOGRAPHS: Cherie Gates 14-15c.

WOODLAND PARK ZOO: Dennis Conner 24br, 25t, 24-25c, 25b.

Special Editions of DK Travel Guides

DK Travel Guides can be purchased in bulk quantities at discounted prices for use in promotions or as premiums. We are also able to offer special editions and personalized jackets, corporate imprints, and excerpts from all of our books, tailored specifically to meet your own needs.

To find out more, please contact:
(in the United States) **SpecialSales@dk.com**
(in the UK) **Sarah.Burgess@dk.com**
(in Canada) DK Special Sales at **general@tourmaline.ca**
(in Australia) **business.development@pearson.com.au**

Selected Street Index